EVEN THE RAIN IS DIFFERENT

D1340457

EVEN THE RAIN
IS DIFFERENT

Edited by

Gwyneth Tyson Roberts

Betty Lane

Elizabeth Harris

Susan Richardson

HONNO AUTOBIOGRAPHY

Published by Honno
'Ailsa Craig', Heol y Cawl, Dinas Powys
Bro Morgannwg, CF6 4AH

First impression 2005

British Library Cataloguing in Publication Data.

A catalogue record for this book is available from the British Library.

ISBN 1 870206 63 0

*Published with the financial support
of the Welsh Books Council*

Cover image: Getty Images/Jules Frazier
Cover design by Chris Lee Design

Typeset and printed in Wales by
Dinefwr Press, Llandybïe.

Contents

Introduction

Travel broadens the mind, and reinforces prejudices; travel brings people of different nations closer, and shows them how far apart they are; travel changes some travellers forever, and leaves others obstinately the same. Even a brief trawl through some of the clichés about travel reminds us that travellers and others use it – and descriptions of it – for their own particular purposes, and that all generalisations about it should be treated with scepticism (including this one). Whatever else, these comments reflect the view that the effects of travel depend at least as much on the personality and frame of mind of the traveller as on details of the peoples and places visited, and it is strongly-contrasting personalities and frames of mind, as well as very different places and peoples, that are represented in this collection of pieces of writing by Welsh women about their experiences abroad.

It was not intended to offer a vast geographical panorama of travel by Welshwomen but the places which were visited range widely, from Southern Europe to Japan, the Middle East to Australia, East Africa to China, the United States to Russia and Ukraine, North Africa to South America and Eastern Europe to India. It was not intended to offer any sort of historical perspective on travel in the twentieth century, either, but one of the pieces begins in 1914, another ends in 2002, and every decade in between is represented; there are also two pieces from the nineteenth century as a brief reminder that Welsh women were travelling the world in earlier periods as well. The range across place and time is entirely down to my good fortune in the pieces of writing which were submitted for the book and those which I found in the National Library of Wales, and I am very grateful not only to all the contributors but also to Gwenllïan Dafydd (General Editor for Honno when I began work on the book) for suggesting that material held in the Manuscript Department could be a valuable source; six pieces included here are adapted from material held there (those by Maureen Bell, Freda Broadbank, Letitia Mary Davies, Joanna Routledge, E. Ann Rutherford and Helen Wareing, which are all taken from Welsh Arts Council MS A1989/23). Chance produced pairs which set each other off: two pieces on New York, for example, in which the writers' reactions to the same city are so different that they seem to epitomise different approaches to travel, and two pieces on Patagonia set nearly 140 years apart, in which the second offers an answer to the question of whether the hopes and ambitions of the community described in the first piece were fulfilled. There are also three pieces on Italy, one treating it as a world heritage site full of artistic and architectural treasures, a second regarding it as the setting for events of Roman history with contemporary relevance, and the third seeing it as the location of the much-loved family home. Experiences of travel are as varied as the travellers.

I had hoped for variety in the pieces I wanted to use; I found even more than I had expected. The contrasts between the pieces of writing I wanted to use were so many and so substantial that it rapidly became clear that my original plan of arranging the pieces to bring out the contrasts between them was likely, over the length of the book, to emphasise the more extreme differences and ignore some of the similarities which made more subtle differences particularly interesting. I felt that a structure which grouped together pieces which shared themes, motives for travel, or approach to their content could enable the variations in theme and content to stand out from each other more clearly and allow for a more nuanced comparison; the terrain travelled by Welshwomen abroad seemed sufficiently varied, in all senses, for signposts to be helpful.

Which leads to a point at which definitions would seem to be in order.

Who is a Welsh woman, what is she?

Welsh identity is a large and complex subject which has been discussed and investigated with varying degrees of rigour and subtlety for many years, and has become a minefield in which only the foolhardy (or obsessed) stomp around without great caution; additional questions raised by gender stereotyping can make definition of a Welsh woman even more problematic. After some consideration of the material I was choosing from I discarded any formal qualification as a criterion: the facts of birth in Wales, Welsh parentage or a certain number of years' residence in Wales were not in themselves any indication that the writer had any particular interest in the country or its people. Eventually I realised that in the most interesting pieces the writers made clear their relation to Wales, although the nature of that relation and the way it was expressed might vary widely, and this became the element in the writing I looked for. I was aware that this was a very broad criterion, but after considerable thought decided that the inclusivity that this allowed for gave an opportunity to reflect the complexity of positions and attitudes in relation to Welshness in a way that a more simplistic approach would not have done; this was important because of the ways in which so many of the pieces addressed the issue of identity, whether directly or by implication. The question of Welshness itself was made inescapably more complex in this context by the fact that, while for many Welsh people part of the definition of being Welsh lies in not being English, Welsh travellers abroad have often found that their Welshness is denied or ignored by the people they are travelling among, not only for legal and diplomatic purposes (their passports say they are British) but because for general purposes all British people are often lumped together under the undifferentiated label of 'English'. In these circumstances, a Welsh woman can find herself in the position of either acquiesing in the label, and thus denying an important element of her identity, or asserting her non-English Welshness in situations where it may cause offence, misunderstanding, or serious – and potentially dangerous – problems.

Where is 'abroad' and how do you know when you've got there?

'Abroad' is one of those words which can only be defined by reference to another: it is necessary to have a concept of 'home country' before you can be 'abroad' from it. There is therefore a sense in which accounts of life and travel abroad make an underlying reference to the country which is the traveller's home – not (or not only) in obvious ways like unfamiliarity of language, currency and customs of the country visited, but in terms of the social and cultural expectations from which she approaches it. At the same time, an account of travel in which the traveller remained emotionally in her own back yard and regarded the rest of the world as quaint little foreigners who only existed in relation to herself and her wishes was not what I had in mind for this book, and I came to realise that what I was really looking for was a sense of engagement with the people, places or culture of the country visited. This is easier to recognise than define, and varies according both to the individual responses of different writers and to factors such as degrees of similarity, between the home and visited countries, of social and cultural structures and a common language, but it seemed to me a prerequisite for a piece of writing which attempted to go any deeper than an entirely factual, 'guidebook', account of a place and its people. It has been suggested that the most satisfying travel writing strikes a balance between factual information and authorial reflection, and it was this balance I was looking for.

It is often said that the best way to make contact with other peoples and cultures is to travel alone, and that travelling or living with compatriots can insulate the traveller from her surroundings (around half the pieces here are by women living or travelling alone). While the advantages are indisputable the disadvantages are equally clear, and some of the pieces here reflect not only the opportunities for closer contact across cultures which travelling solo can bring, but also some of the difficulties, frustrations and dangers which can arise in societies which regard it as entirely reasonable for a man to travel on his own but make immediate assumptions about the social status and sexual availability of the lone female traveller, who may then be driven into forms of behaviour she would not have chosen for herself entirely in order to avoid the problems which asserting her own tastes and wishes – that is, aspects of her own personal identity – could bring. Although certainly such difficulties and dangers can be overemphasised: Jan

Morris, a Welsh woman whose experience of travel is considerably wider and more varied than most, feels that women travellers have the edge, writing: *I have had the peculiar experience of travelling both as a man and as a woman, and I have reached the conclusion, on the whole, that during my own travelling years the female has had it easier than the male.* (Her reasons are that women travellers were more likely to be helped and protected by the host communities she visited.) In other cases having a detailed knowledge of the forms of behaviour acceptable to the people you are travelling among can take you a long way (often literally) , as sometimes can a (genuine or carefully cultivated) air of naïve goodwill and general cluelessness, but both have their limitations; sometimes travellers find it a relief to focus for a time on the place rather than the people.

One of the elements which runs through many of these pieces is delight in the natural world; they are full of descriptions of and references to landscapes, plants, birds and animals (especially but not only when they are travelling through the countryside). This loving awareness of the natural world produces some of the most vivid and colourful passages against which human society is sometimes shown as being frustrating, unsympathetic or difficult to understand as well as endlessly fascinating, and some of the most effective of these passages work by (sometimes implied) reference to the natural world of Wales. Scenes from a film which show a pale blue sky and a bare tree silhouetted against a weak winter sun take a Welsh woman in Australia home to Wales in her mind; a Welsh woman in Michigan contrasts its endless horizons with the green hills and trees which bound the views she is accustomed to in Wales; returning with her father from her first visit to Italy – the home of his family and of the culture she was brought up in – to a rain-soaked August day in Wales, a Welsh woman reflects, in the words that give this book its title, that *even the rain seemed cruelly different*. Seeing other countries can make it possible to see Wales itself more clearly.

It can also offer the possibility of seeing oneself more clearly. Travel has traditionally given travellers the chance to make themselves into someone new, breaking (or at least cracking) the mould into which the demands and constraints of their life at home – family, friends, job, social class – have forced them to fit; it can also be the occasion for travellers to recognise aspects of their personalities which were less obvious against the backdrop of their habitual life at home and which they were not previously aware of, and thus give them a clearer sense of who they are. In a letter to her lover from Baghdad Gertrude Bell, the traveller and archaeologist, wrote: *I have seen and heard strange things and they colour the mind . . . Don't . . . tell anyone that the me they knew will not come back in the me that returns.* (This and the comments from Jan Morris are both taken from *Off the Beaten Track: Three Centuries of Women Travellers* by Dea Birkett, 2004.) This awareness of change in oneself is present in pieces here which describe the writers' visits to countries with which they have close ties of family, culture, language or religion, and can be seen as the underlying theme of many other pieces also; it is often by contact with other (as well as 'Other') identities that the writers' sense of their own identity becomes at least clearer, and often more secure.

Equally, this exposure to different ways of looking at the world and the travellers' response to them can also create moments of heightened awareness which remain for some writers among the most important of their experiences of travelling abroad: a feeling of living through moments suspended in time, a sense of total and all-pervading inner peace, a sudden awareness of being this person and no other, in this place and no other, at this time and no other. This too can be part of the effect of travelling which enables travellers to feel that they see and know themselves better, and for many travellers, including perhaps the writers here who describe such moments, it is this sort of experience, as much as curiosity about other peoples and places, that makes them want to go on travelling. Perhaps, after all, some journeys *can* change some travellers for ever. Some journeys. Some travellers. And perhaps.

Gwyneth Tyson Roberts
2005

I

WANDERING FREE

Visiting another country only and entirely because that is where you want to be is often regarded as the purest form of travel and, whereas some of the other chapters describe the experiences of Welsh women who had specific and practical reasons for travelling, this chapter contains accounts of travel made with less direct and easily-identified aims. The women who wrote these pieces were impelled to travel from curiosity about the place they visited (Patagonia), because of the vague possibility of a job there that might give them a more interesting life than the one they had had in Britain (Tunisia), or bcause of a man who offered a new and different way of life that might bring a greater chance of happiness (Corsica). Although their motives were different, they shared freedom of choice in where they went and what they did when they got there.

The visit to Patagonia gave an opportunity for the writer to convince herself through her own experience that a community which had seemed to her so improbable as to be almost mythical actually existed; she found not only that the people were real but that she had met one of them already, while she seemed at least as unreal to another as he did to her. The Welsh woman in Tunisia who made her way to a travel agents' in Hammamet was so convinced that a job there offered by the casual remark of a stranger met in a Fishguard pub was real and would be held open for her that she did not have enough money for the return fare; she found that neither the job nor the stranger was waiting for her, but discovered a totally unexpected compatriot. The third piece is an account of an inner journey as much as a description of the writer's life in Corsica; by the end of her time there she felt as trapped, in a different way, as she had at the beginning of her account, when a new life in Corsica had seemed to offer freedom.

The piece on Patagonia focuses on elements outside the writer (the people she met, the stories they had to tell, and the variety and beauty of the changing colours of the landscape), while the other two pieces show much less interest in the people of the places the writers are visiting. The Tunisians are shown as either aggressively unpleasant or unsympathetic, while the Corsicans are seen only from the point of view of whether they were obstructive or helpful to the writer and her partner; the contrast between the way they are presented in this piece and the way the Patagonians are described in the first piece is particularly telling.

These pieces show a wide range of motives for the journeys they describe and in the writers' expectations about what they would find there, as well as a wide range of responses to the people and experiences which the journeys brought to the writers. If they have one thing in common, it is perhaps that they suggest that motives for travel often have less to do with 'pure' curiosity than the travellers may think at the time.

Ym Mhatagonia

IMOGEN RHIA HERRAD

April 2002, Gaiman

On the outskirts of the small town of Gaiman big hoard-ings advertise Welsh tea-shops, Tŷ Nain and Tŷ Te Cymreig and Tŷ Gwyn (respectively, 'Grandmother's House', 'Welsh Tea-shop', and 'White House'). Then a wide, empty main road, crossed by narrower side streets: everything dry, dusty. Most of the houses are nondescript although some are startlingly white or elaborately built of red brick. The whole town – village, really – looks empty; there's the odd car on the road and one or two people, and dogs sleeping in the shade, but those few figures are swallowed up by the vast land and sky.

The taxi slows down, avoids a large pothole in the road and turns right into one of the dusty side-streets. We drive towards the whitish hill at the end of the road. There's a sign on the left: B&B *Gwesty Tywi* (Tywi Hotel). The air smells dusty and dry and clean, all at the same time. The sun is hot.

The first thing I see as we go inside the house is a big chair against the wall on the right. *Y gwir yn erbyn y byd* is carved into its back around the figure of a dragon: 'the truth against the world', the motto of the Gorsedd of Bards. We pass through an archway and into the parlour, the centrepiece of which is a beautiful Welsh dresser.

It is hard to believe that I am in Argentina.

October 1989, Aberystwyth

I have just spent the summer in Wales on an intensive Welsh course in Lampeter. One night someone mentions a forthcoming talk about Patagonia and the Welsh-speaking community there. I find it very hard to believe that there are Welsh speakers at the very end of South America; I imagine them as strange mythical people on old maps of countries that no one has ever come back from.

I can't go to the talk, but at some point I decide that I want to go to Patagonia. I am still not entirely convinced that either the place or its Welsh speakers exist.

April 2002, Gaiman

I am staying in the B&B run by Gwyn and Mónica Jones. Mónica is a poet who writes in Welsh and Spanish; last year she won the Chair (the highest honour) for the best Welsh-language poem in blank verse at the Patagonian Eisteddfod: this was the chair I noticed on entering the house. The Welsh dresser was her grandmother's; she had it shipped over all the way from Wales!

I go to my room and unpack. Doors and windows are open, outside is hot and sunny. It feels like summer to me and I can't quite grasp the fact that here it's autumn.

I walk by the river, where the air is close and hot and full of the whirring of mosquito wings and unknown bird calls, to *Casa de Té Tŷ Nain* ('tea-shop' in Spanish plus 'grand-mother's house' in Welsh). I have heard that in the tea-shop there is a small exhibition about the first Welsh settlers; that's why I want to come here first.

The door is locked, but a faded handwritten sign says – I think – *Please ring bell* in Spanish. I ring. Some time later the door is opened by a woman with black and white hair, an apron and a slow smile.

I explain that I'm interested in the history of the Welsh settlers. And in a cup of tea.

'Of course,' she says. 'Come in!'

She bustles off, and I can hear banging and rattling of crockery; two grandfather clocks tick loudly. Then loudspeakers crackle and a Welsh choir bursts into song.

It is cool indoors after the heat outside. The air smells a little dusty, as in a secondhand book shop. The walls are covered with old photographs, assorted tools and two ancient telephones (the first in Patagonia, a sign next to them proclaims proudly). By the door is a complicated family tree – framed – going back to Welsh ancestors and including the places they came from. Having ancestors who came over on the *Mimosa*, the ship carrying the first settlers from Wales in 1865, appears to be important.

The woman, carrying a large teapot in a hand-crocheted red tea-cosy, comes back followed by her husband. They introduce themselves as Mirna Jones de Ferrari and Rubén Ferrari. He doesn't speak much Welsh, she explains, but knows a lot about the history of the Welsh in Argentina. She bustles off and returns with a laden tray.

'This,' she says, 'is *teisen du* (black cake), fruit cake with raisins soaked in brandy. Very nice. There's a cream cake with chocolate – the Welsh like sweet things, you know. Then there's apple pie, lemon tart and scones. And bread and butter, of course.'

We talk about the Welsh in Gaiman.

'When I first went to primary school,' says Mirna in Spanish, 'I was six years old and I could only speak Welsh.'

'*Todo Cymraeg!*' Rubén confirms ('everything' in Spanish, 'Welsh-language' in Welsh).

'But you were born here?' I ask, confused.

'Oh yes,' she says. 'I grew up on my parents' farm. We only spoke Welsh there.'

'My great-grandfather,' says Rubén, not wanting to be left out, 'came here from *Maes Môn*. Is it called that? In the north. An island.' He thinks. 'Anglesey.'

'*Ynys Môn*,' I say.

'That's it!' He is relieved. 'John Tomos Jones was his name. He came over in 1874. I've got an uncle in Anglesey still, John Lazarus Williams. I don't really speak Welsh, but I sing in it. The Welsh have such beautiful, lively songs!' He laughs.

'Oh please,' I say, 'sing one. Please!'

Eventually he gives in ('But don't tell anyone in the town!') and sings *Mochyn du* in a beautiful baritone.

Somewhat dazed by this display of Welshness, I ask if they feel themselves to be Welsh or Argentinian.

'We're Argentinian,' Rubén says forcefully. '¡*Somos argentinos*! But! But, we know what life was like for our ancestors in Wales and we still have some customs here that have died out long since in Wales. We're Argentinians of Welsh extraction, and proud of it. We have our history, the wonderful history of the Welsh colony.'

'*Cymry yn y galon*,' says Mirna. We're Welsh in our hearts.

'*En la sangre!*' Rubén proclaims passionately. In our blood.

We have another cup of tea, then Mirna shows me round the exhibition. 'These came over on the *Mimosa*,' she says. 'These' are a pair of china dogs. 'They were a wedding present. My husband's great-grandmother brought them over.'

I try to imagine that. The first people who came over into the unknown, a vast region many times the size of Britain where no other Europeans lived, had left all the familiar things of Wales behind. It must have comforted the young bride to take these two fragile symbols of civilisation with her into the untamed and unknown wilderness.

Several hours pass before I get up to leave. Mirna refuses to accept any money for the wonderful cakes and tea. 'No, no, no,' she says, 'we've had such a lovely afternoon. You'll pay next time. When you come back next year!'

We spend half an hour saying goodbye; finally, I'm outside on the road again. I feel dazed. It's only a few hours since I arrived in Patagonia, alone and somewhat lost in this large foreign country; now, after an afternoon of Welsh tea and conversation, I feel as if I'd spent days here. Gaiman, partly Welsh and wholly Argentinian, is still as strange but not as foreign as before.

The next morning I walk down the *Calle Miguel D. Jones* – Michael D. Jones of Bala was one of the leading figures behind the founding of the Welsh settlement in Patagonia – on my way to Coleg Camwy (*Dyffryn Camwy* is the Welsh name for the Chubut valley). An elderly man and a youth are about to clear bushes from the footpath of dry beaten earth which leads to the school building, of red brick with sash windows – very unusual in Argentina. There is a slightly rusty sign in Spanish: *Primera escuela secundaria de la Patagonia, fundada en 1906* (the first secondary school in Patagonia, founded in 1906). A plaque on the side of the building says *Nid Byd, Byd Heb Wybodaeth* in Welsh (the world could not exist without education) and *La Educación es el Pan del Alma* in Spanish (education is the food of the soul).

Gabro is the Welsh teacher – from Gaiman, but he too learned most of his Welsh on a course in Lampeter. At the end of the lesson he tells me more: 'Since 1996 Welsh has been part of the curriculum in Coleg Camwy, the only secondary school in Argentina where this is so. In the eighth grade pupils choose between French and Welsh as their first foreign language. Last year, thirty-one of the thirty-five chose Welsh. In the afternoons I teach in a primary school outside Gaiman, in Bryngwyn, and I teach evening classes as well.' He says that some but not all of the Welsh learners have a Welsh speaker in the family – more often a grandparent than a parent.

A couple of hours later we are in his car on the way to Bryngwyn, and he tells me about the primary school. 'Welsh lessons were started by the previous head teacher – a Welsh-speaker – but she retired two years ago and her successor came from the very north of Argentina and didn't even know what the Welsh language was when she arrived. The parents were very unhappy at losing the Welsh lessons for their children, and one day I got a phone call from her asking me to continue them. Last year the provincial government stopped the extra money for Welsh teaching but she managed to get it somewhere else so the children can still learn Welsh.'

The river valley is beautifully green; the air is cooler than in Gaiman, but just as dry. To the left of the road as we approach Bryngwyn is an old Welsh chapel: weirdly familiar and yet somehow also out of place. The school stands to its right, another beautiful red-brick building. With sash windows.

After the lesson I meet the head teacher, the new one from the north who once didn't know what Welsh was; she is surprisingly young and clearly very competent. She tells me that about 40 per cent of the children in Bryngwyn primary school learn Welsh, most of them coming from farms scattered across the countryside. Many of them are Bolivians who only speak Quitchua at home, the language of the Incas, and their parents are among the most enthusiastic that their children should learn Welsh, English and other languages, hoping that they will later be able to get work in the tourist industry – which brings the danger that Quitchua may end up here with the same low status of a 'peasant' and 'backward' language which Welsh once had in Wales. Fifty years ago Welsh was thought as unnecessary in Patagonia as it was in Wales, but *la sangre*, as Rubén said yesterday, is still important. The cities of Trelew and Porth

Madryn near Gaiman are full of people who will tell you proudly that they are of Welsh descent even though the language died out there two or three generations ago.

Blood and ancestry are clearly important in other ways too: the Quitchua speakers look markedly different from the descendants of the Welsh settlers, and however many languages they learn their indigenous origins will still leave them open to prejudice and discrimination. The Tehuelche, who once lived in the Chubut valley, have been almost completely wiped out.

The following morning I walk to the Gaiman cemetery to look at the graves.The street are empty so early in the morning. As I walk, the black night slowly becomes inky blue. The eastern sky in front of me turns silver; behind me, to the west, all is still dark. I am cold in the dawn wind and tired, but elated. There is no sound apart from the rustling of the trees in the wind and my own footsteps. The eastern sky slowly catches fire. By the time I arrive at the grave-yard gates the sun is just coming up in the valley, its first rays warm on my wind-cold face.

The cemetery is much larger than I expected. Some of the inscriptions are entirely in Welsh, some in Spanish, one or two in English; several record Welsh names in the middle of Spanish inscriptions. Some of the headstones are dark and seem somehow familiar: made of slate, I realise. I didn't know there was slate in Patagonia. Then I read the words on the side: *Morgan a'i Fab, Bala*. Shipped over from Wales, like the dressers and the china dogs, by the early settlers and their children. I wonder about them: were they homesick? Did the children born in Patagonia think of Wales as Home? Or were they already Patagonians with a love of the warm, dry climate, the constant whistling wind and the land's many shades of brown and gold?

I go to town, looking for the *Locutorio*, a sort of cybercafécum-long-distance-phone shop. All the signs on the walls are in Spanish and the woman behind the counter doesn't look at all Welsh. I take a deep breath and trot out my most fluent sentence in Spanish: '*Por favor,¿habla usted galés?*' Do you speak Welsh, please?

And she answers '*Tipyn bach.*' A little. Her name is Noemí Lloyd and she grew up on a farm called Bethesda, near Bryngwyn. She says she speaks Welsh because she works in the phone shop; many Welsh people come in wanting to phone home. She spoke Welsh as a child at home, later forgot most of it, and is now studying it at evening classes in Coleg Camwy (it is the only foreign language taught there). She is a member of one of the five choirs in Gaiman – one male, one female, one mixed and two children's – and tonight is choir-practice. I decide to go.

Two middle-aged ladies – both Welsh speakers – sit to my right and left. Someone hands me a sheet of music. And they're off. I close my eyes and feast my ears.

April 2002, in the middle of nowhere
I am on the long-distance coach that goes from the Atlantic coast to Esquél and the Andes mountain range, 400 miles away. It leaves Gaiman at one in the afternoon and reaches Esquél at nine: eight hours of the pampas.

The sky is deeply and intensely blue. At first, in the valley of the River Chubut, there is a lot of green – grass, trees, bushes – but as we get into the pampas proper the earth gets darker and drier, and everything is in shades of brown: gold, yellow, ochre, copper, sepia.

Hours later strange rock formations appear on the horizon: *Los Altares*, *Yr Allorau* – the altars – given their names by Welsh settlers who travelled from Gaiman into the unknown a hundred years ago. They are three columns of rock, striped grey and brown as if someone had painted them. I wish I could walk for a few hours in the clear blue air, in the cool whistling wind and the hot sunshine, surrounded by the unbroken silence. I wish I could make this journey by car, or on horseback, at the same pace as the first European travellers; or on foot like the Tehuelche whose land this was for centuries, so that I could see the land as they did, slowly, slowly: the world filled with silence, the blues and golds and browns of the days and the absolute, star-encrusted blackness of the nights.

It is almost dusk; the shadows are long and the light has turned from gold to purple when we stop in the middle of nowhere. Three people and a horse stand by the roadside.

I rub my eyes. A horse, and three gauchos. Two of them get on the coach; with them comes a smell of wood-smoke and horses and leather. The third mounts the horse and rides off into the sunset.

One of the two gauchos on the coach wears a hard flat black hat of the kind that previously I've only seen on photos with the caption *Typical Argentinian gaucho* underneath. I try to get a better look at him without seeming to stare. I've never seen a real gaucho before.

He turns round, scanning the other passengers. Then he notices me. He sees my eyebrows (green) and my hair (henna'ed with a blue strand). He stares and stares. He clearly can't believe it. He's probably never seen anyone with blue hair and green eyebrows before. He goes on staring.

We'll both have a story to tell now.

I have crossed a continent in one day; from Esquél it's only another fifty miles or so to the Pacific coast. Suddenly civilisation bursts in from all sides. It's only Esquél Coach Terminal, but it comes as a shock after a day filled with nothing but far horizons.

Someone is calling out my name. It's Rini Griffiths,

whom I last saw two years ago on the Eisteddfod field in Llanelli.

'What a surprise!' she says, and gives me a hug. 'Mónica from Gaiman only told me to meet someone off the coach, she didn't say it was you! Good to see you.'

We drive to her house, which is outside the town. The air is much colder here than in Gaiman.

The next morning I get up very early and go outside. It's cold and damp; there's a smell of pine trees and wet earth in the air.

Esquél lies in the valley below, hidden in a cloud of mist. Beyond it are the Andes, massive brown stone crags topped with snow. The sun comes up behind them and turns the mist into shimmering silver.

Trying My Luck in Tunisia

HAYLEY LONG

I strode purposefully down the busy main street, ignoring the stares of the local men on their mopeds. They were applying their brakes with reckless abandon in order to catch a better glimpse of the small white girl who walked alone, half-buried under the weight of her enormous backpack.

'*Aslammah.*'

Keeping my eyes fixed firmly ahead of me, I continued to walk. I'd been around a bit by now; these guys didn't worry me.

'*Aslammah* bay-bee. You speak Inglish? Français? Deutsch?'

A quick glance out of the corner of my eye told me that there were now three of them trailing me slowly along the kerb on perilously-clapped out mopeds. Oil from one bike was dripping at an alarming rate and mingling unpleasantly with the litter and spit and camel-shit which had already found their resting-places in the gutter.

Unhappily for me, my observation was detected and interpreted as a sign of interest. The men began to shout and whistle and pester me some more as I marched briskly onwards, still desperately feigning ignorance of their existence (with decreasing success). I tried to think of something else. And I managed to. I thought about the fact that somewhere deep under the horrid weight of my wretched backpack, sweat was being generated with incredible

13

efficiency and was now dripping steadily down my back and collecting in my soaking knickers.

'You speek Ing-leesh?'

These guys were persistent; some kind of response was in order. Without slackening my pace I turned my head ever so slightly, gave a vague smile, and shook my head with calculated incomprehension. The moped men looked interested.

'*Sprechen sie Deutsch*?'

I began to count my steps to see if this would help me ignore them.

'*Parlez-vous Français*?'

Six. Seven. Eight. My mind began to race ahead of me. Nine. Ten. Eleven. They didn't worry *me*. I'd been all over the place. Twelve. Thirteen. I'd done America single-handed, for God's sake. Fourteen. But I still needed to say something quickly to get rid of these idiots on bikes. Fifteen. The answer came in a flash. Abruptly, I stopped walking and turned to face the three laughing men with a sly smile of my own.

'*Ydych chi'n siarad Cymraeg*?' (Do you speak Welsh?)

The laughter stopped and the buzzing engines fell silent. I asked the question again, louder and with more confidence. '*Ydych chi'n siarad Cymraeg*?'

The nearest man frowned and bowed a little under my gaze. To my relief I felt my breathing begin to relax at the same pace my elation was growing. The Tunisians exchanged uncertain glances before looking back at me, suddenly at a loss for words. I shrugged with boredom and tossed my chin into the air.

'*Dim ots!*' (Doesn't matter!)

Sitting speechless on their mopeds, the men watched as I readjusted my pack and marched off down the road away from them.

I found the office quite easily; it nestled between two similar offices, and the little parade of shops looked incongruous against the decrepit hovels which lined the sides of the Rue Däg Hammerskjoeld. But then everything about the street was absurd – not least its name, which suggested Scandinavian cleanliness and order rather than the obstacle-course of filth and camel-dung I had just made my way through. I took a deep breath, crossed my fingers and pushed my way through the door.

It was dark and messy inside the office, but it seemed like a haven after the street. Across the back wall of the room ran a large formica-topped table at which a dark-skinned woman sat and typed on a manual typewriter. She looked up at me and frowned, just as the men had when I spoke in Welsh. Her frown was unnecessary: I had no intention of speaking the old language now.

'I'm looking for Larry.'

'He doesn't work here.'

This time it was my turn to freeze. 'Pardon?'

'He doesn't work here.' She turned away and went on with her typing. This was bad. So I was confident. So I had been around. But this was still *very* bad.

'There must be some mistake,' I said, feeling the sweat beginning to slide off my forehead as well as my back. 'I'm quite sure I've come to the right place.'

The girl looked at me and raised her eyebrows in a bored gesture of annoyance. 'Wait here,' she said in heavily-accented English. 'I'll go and find my boss.'

She disappeared through a back door and left me to sit down on a plastic-seated chair and look around. I was in a cheap, untidy office, cluttered with files and piles of holiday brochures. On the walls, blue seas and pristine white buildings sparkled back at me from posters with the legend *Tunisia*. It didn't look much like the place that I had so far encountered; since my arrival in the country four hours before I had only seen grubby buildings and grubbier roads. On the other side of the office window was the legendary Rue Däg Hammerskjoeld that Larry had told me about that night in the pub in Fishguard – filthy, stinking and hazardous.

I wiped my forehead with a tissue and scraped my hair back into a tight ponytail. A few months earlier I had allowed one of the girls living in the Fishguard hostel to chop it all off, but it was already growing back to a length which was proving difficult. I tucked my backpack under the plastic chair and hoped that the manager, whoever he or she was, wouldn't notice it. I desperately needed to create a good impression, and the last thing I wanted was for this manager person to think I was some nutty back-packing idiot who had just walked in on the offchance of the casual promise of a job while drinking in a West Wales pub. I delved into my pocket for some lipstick but realised with disappointment that it had completely melted, leaving nothing but a sticky red residue in the lining of my shorts. I felt my spirits and my body slump.

'My name is Suzie Chanelle. I'm in charge here. How can I help you?' The sharp South Walian voice almost made me jump off my chair. After a split-second delay in which I decided she came from Neath, I collected my wits and sprang forward to shake her hand.

'I'm Elli Jones. I was given this address and told to ask for Larry . . .' For a moment I faltered helplessly and then added, rather lamely, 'er . . . I was hoping to speak to Larry.' It suddenly struck me that I had just travelled all the way to Hammamet, Tunisia, in the hope of being given a job by someone whose surname I didn't even know. My spirits sank further. I *was* a nutty, backpacking idiot.

Suzie Chanelle, a tall angular woman with very blue

eyes and an expression of subtle contempt, regarded me coolly. 'The man you are looking for is Larry Disario and he no longer works for this company. His contract was terminated following a few rather embarrassing investigations. If it's a job you're after, I certainly wouldn't recommend that you quote Mr Disario's name as a referee.'

'Oh . . .'

Shit. Shit. I didn't have a Plan B. I didn't even have enough money to fly back home. She *had* to give me a job. I tried a new tack.

'Look,' I said, sitting back on the plastic chair, 'I know I sound like an idiot, but the thing is . . . ' I leaned forward and lowered my voice so that the sultry Tunisian receptionist I had spoken to earlier wouldn't hear,'. . . the thing is . . . I *really* need a job . . .' Suzie Chanelle raised her eyebrows. I lowered my voice even more: '. . . and I'll work like an absolute bastard.'

For a second I thought I saw the flicker of a smile cross her face. I held her gaze and kept my face deadly serious. I had one last desperate card to play.

'*Cymru am byth*,' I whispered. Wales for ever.

Suzie Chanelle glowered down at me and then, all of a sudden, burst into a dry throaty laugh. I remained rigid, not daring to relax until I had heard her next words.

'A free spirit has blown into my camp, has it? Well, we'll see how this free spirit shapes up in an electric-blue Rep's uniform. I am making a *huge* exception for you – my staff generally reach me after a very rigid selection procedure in Britain. You're on strict probation – if you don't shape up at any time, you're straight out, *Cymru* or no *Cymru*. I'm not sentimental. Do you understand me?'

I exhaled slowly. 'Absolutely.'

Now I could relax.

Down and Out in Corsica

JOANNA ROUTLEDGE

I married young and divorced a few years later; there were no children. I then qualified as a social worker. In the late 1970s I moved with Brendan, the man I was living with, to Wales and we rented a farmhouse at the end of a long track. Here I enjoyed milking goats, feeding chickens, making lots of good produce, and generally having a taste of 'the good life'.

1981 was a big changing-point in my life: my father died unexpectedly, Brendan and I split up, and I moved into the first of many temporary homes. My itinerant life-style began at this point. I have always wanted to be as close to Nature as possible; Nature has been my friend and solace when humans have failed me. Not wanting to return to social work, which had left me disillusioned, I went on a course in silk-screen printing and found a new base to my life. But my need for adventure was strong, and in Spring 1983 I went to France with my rucksack on my back, looking for fruit-picking work. I felt young and strong and had always been used to hard physical work. Fate took me to the Dordogne, picking strawberries.

The family I worked for introduced me to an Englishman they knew who lived nearby, Martin (pronounced 'Martan'). I fell in love with this crazy guy and his long blond hair and violet-blue eyes. He had been an architect and enjoyed designing and building different outdoor shelters which were sculptures in wood. We were both ready for a 'holi-day', and Martin had just finished building a gypsy-style caravan in beautiful willow wood. He planned to take it to Corsica, where he had previously lived; he invited me to go with him. I dithered, but not for too long. I decided to go with him, and rushed back to Wales to organise my departue.

I gave up the cottage I was living in, gave away all my material possessions to my friends, packed up a car-load of belongings and zoomed off. From Joan I had become Joanna and 'Laughing Water', a name Martin gave me which I loved. We lived in his green tent in a shady glade. I swam in a red-clay pool and began to talk to trees and shake off the dust of civilisation and respectability. My life before I went to live with Martin would already have been described as 'uncivilised' by many people: no inside loo, no inside tap, no running hot water, no central heating, always living on the breadline. I had already started living closer to Nature in the farmhouse in Wales. As with everything else, I went further with Martin. I was so conscious of the nuclear threat that I couldn't understand how Martin could be so unconcernedly out of touch with what was going on in the world at large, or how he could have forgotten his first language through having lived in French-speaking countries for so long. I also did not realise his weakness for wine.

I loved Corsica instantly: the seas, the skies, the sun, the moon and the stars, the shapes and forms of trees and stones. The cork trees were so weird, the chestnut trees so enormous, and the old eucalyptus trees so graceful.

Martin had been receiving Unemployment Benefit in France, but it took several weeks for it to be transferred to Corsica. He had spent the last of his money on our tickets, and I had none left. We camped by the sea, got food vouchers from a Catholic charity and scavenged at the local market, picking up the boxes of stuff that the stall-holders were about to throw away at closing-time. Eventually the money came through and we headed for the mountains. I found an empty shepherds' hut high up, where it was really bleak. We decided to leave the caravan and car below, and to spend the winter in the hut.

The peasants in the mountains burn out holes in the centre of some of the old chestnut trees, and the hollow trees become shelter for pigs when they are turned out on to the mountains in December. Trees like these have a weird shape and an atmosphere about them which I love. The first time I slept in one I woke to the sound of hooves, looked up and saw the face of a man on a horse looking down through the hole in the tree at me still in bed. I wonder what he thought: 'crazy foreigners', probably.

Moving up the mountain was hard work; the sacks of potatoes and other food supplies had to be carried on our backs. Apples were also in season, and we carried up bagfuls. Apples, potatoes and chestnuts were our main diet. I remember eating a sausage (I hadn't eaten meat for years), dripping the piping hot fat into stale white French bread over a fire as we ate with peasants after picking chestnuts with them. The hut wasn't protected by any trees and was very exposed to the elements. I enjoyed the isolation, but Martin found it too bleak. In the end the mountain police came to tell us that it would be too dangerous to our lives for us to stay there in winter, and that we would have to leave. So all the sacks of potatoes that we'd so laboriously hauled up the mountain had to be hauled down again.

My car was already much tattier than when she'd set out, as was her owner. Martin found some tubes of brightly-coloured dyes on one of the rubbish-tips and, thinking that they were paints, covered the car in bizarre colours and patterns. The following day the 'paint' was still wet and when after several days we re-read the instructions we discovered that the dye would remain wet for ever. Every time we touched the car we were covered with blue, green, red or yellow dye, which was oil-based and could not be removed. It was impossible to prevent Maurice the dog from rubbing against the car and he became a real striped wonder. The mountain track had changed to mud and water with the onset of winter, and the car couldn't pull the caravan down the steep track. The village people were so keen to get rid of us gypsies that the snow-plough was authorised to help us.

My cat, Pussywillow, died that winter; I think she got too cold in the mountains and died of hypothermia. I feel so sad about her death, because I think I could have prevented it. Martin and I were always in conflict over feeding the animals; he thought they should find their own food, but since they were already domesticated my view was that we had a responsibility to help them. We had so many arguments over this that in the end I let Martin have his way, and Pussywillow died.

I needed to unload and feel lighter. Before we were towed down the mountain I had made an enormous fire to burn my photos and a large box of my writings. Martin didn't understand, and I didn't expect him to. I see it now as a time of necessary destruction which alone could lead to a rebirth, but knowing that this was inevitable didn't make it easier. I was by now lighter in a material sense also; the trunk of books I'd saved to study during the winter had been stolen, probably because the trunk was of good quality. I tried not to be angry or upset, but it was hard to come to terms with it. Only six months earlier I had left my cottage in Wales where all my treasures had been safe around me.

Christmas 1983 was a subdued affair: Martin had been stabbed in the arm in a drunken brawl in Ajaccio, which I fortunately didn't witness. I had no money, and I felt insignificant and powerless in a world that was founded on money. I once went into a baker's shop to ask if there was any bread from the day before that I could have free; the kind lady gave me a fresh loaf that I didn't have to pay for. I then went to a local supermarket and stole cheese and chocolate to eat with it; what a feast it was! Around the same time I saw a man in the street flicking through the notes in his wallet and very nearly asked him for some money. How near I was to begging, and what a victim I had become.

Natural food is abundant in Corsica and we ate a lot of it: fern shoots, wild strawberries, wild asparagus, figs, cherries, lemons, grapefruit and a lovely red fruit called *arbuse*. We ate nuts and berries, tasted flowers and cooked the roots of some plants.

Eventually we went to the south of Corsica where Raymond, an old friend of Martin, let us live in a chalet he owned near the beach, where we were surrounded by the chanting of frogs. Nearby were the tips, where we and local families did a lot of our 'shopping': stock past its sell-by date from the supermarkets, cheeses, yoghurts, frozen meat and fish. I was accustomed to getting all my clothes from the tip, but getting our food there finished me off. The last straw was one day when I went foraging for food on the tip to find that a hundred pigs were being allowed to roam freely over it. I felt in competition with them: together we milled around, all pushing and snorting and squealing for food. My self-respect plummeted. At this point I had lived with Martin for almost a year, alone with him for most of the time. I was lonely and desperately unhappy, but unable to get myself together to do anything about it.

It was now hot summer. On the tip we found a boat and a windsurfer, crystal stones and leather wallets. The boat was heavy but good fun; we would sail down the river and into the sea. Maurice the dog came with us, rather warily. At this point we lived in the open a lot, making camp under a eucalyptus tree by the river. I became increasingly aware that my quality of life had to change, but felt too trapped inside to make a move.

I was hassled a great deal by men who obviously thought from my life-style that I was promiscuous. Martin had given his car away, not wanting the responsibility, and I had to hitch everywhere; men thought I was on the road looking to earn money. The police were a hassle too, judging us on our appearance and itinerant life-style. Once they came to visit us because a nearby holiday home had been broken into, and took away the boxes of sweets which Martin had found on the tip, saying they had to be analysed for drugs, although I suspect they ended up with the officers' children

After a particularly violent episode with Martin I borrowed some money and returned to Britain, staying with my sister for six weeks. Being in a city depressed me even more; I couldn't find my place with the people or the environment. It was grey and I didn't fit in. It was then fifteen months since I had left Wales and my quality of life had declined on all levels: mentally, emotionally, physically and spiritually. I remember feeling sick and saying to myself, 'It's OK, I need to be sick . . .' I wanted to vomit up the life behind me. I went back to Corsica, but after another violent episode with Martin, I needed to get away from him. I started to look seriously for work and Raymond, who owned the beach chalet, offered me some cleaning work in a house on a hill which overlooked the beach where I had lived with Martin, and lent me a flat. However, at five o'clock one morning Raymond appeared at the flat and told me to be ready to leave that evening as he would be coming to take me to a campsite he owned. I didn't know what he had in mind and panicked when he locked the door behind him. I broke the lock with a knife and fled down the hill to Claudie, whom I had got to know through the cleaning work.

I went to live in her outhouse and then renewed contact with Martin, who was trying to drink less. I began to spend more time with him, especially after he built me a tree-house. It was in a beautiful big olive tree, the symbol of peace. There was a ladder up to the first floor, where Martin cooked on a stove, and on the second floor was the bed, which overlooked the beach and the sea. We would wake in the mornings with sunshine and birds on the bed.

In the summer of 1985 we moved together to the region of La Castagnaccia, a place full of mountain magic and chestnut trees, staying in the isolated and abandoned hamlet of Osio. The air was full of quietness broken only by the tinkling bells of the mountain goats and the calling of the mules to one another. Only elderly people lived in the surrounding villages; the younger ones had moved to the mainland in search of work and life. There were no buses, no trains, no transport of any kind.

We lived in a tall grey crumbling house; nearby was an ancient spring, its water fizzy with iron. Here I found crystals growing on stones, and enormous gnarled old trees. We slept at the top of the house, which had been used to smoke chestnuts dry before they were ground into flour at the nearby mill.

Martin found casual work in the nearby village, gardening or building, and I had an occasional house-cleaning job. I felt lonely, depressed and isolated. I enjoyed living so close to the elements, but I also very much needed the warmth of human contact and intellectual stimulation. I had good moments with Martin, but the ugliness of previous experiences with him had left too many scars and I couldn't trust him. He continued to try to make me happy, living in fear that I would leave and he would be alone again; he was terribly alone.

It became increasingly obvious that I wasn't well. My energy was very low, and the slightest physical activity was becoming an effort and struggle. I knew my health was affected and that I would have to return to the UK to sort out my body and put my life in order. I felt as dry as an empty well, and totally drained of life-force. I knew something was wrong.

A return to the UK in the spring of 1986 for the funeral of my mother's second husband showed me just how far I'd gone from the norms of 'civilised' society. During the visit a cervical smear was taken and I was told I would need further tests. I started to move from Corsica to France, nearer to a return to Wales. I knew I had to put my life in order as well as my health, but I could not accept the idea of staying long in the UK. In December 1986 a repeat smear done in France showed up cancerous cells and I was advised to have a hysterectomy immediately, so I returned to the care of my family and friends in the UK almost four years after my initial departure to pick fruit in France. The things that have happened to me have had a profound influence on me, and I have learned a lot; I feel a spiritually richer and wiser woman for having lived them. My life has made me what I am and in spite of everything I can truly say that I regret nothing.

II

STUDYING

Studying provides not only a clearly-defined reason for travelling but also a clear structure to the time spent in the country visited, whether the structure is imposed by others (as in the account here of an art history course in Florence) or by the traveller's own academic interests (as in the account of a visit to China by the student doing post-graduate work in Chinese archaeology). The writers' specialist knowledge and interests determine not only where they want to go and what they want to see but also their response to what they find there; the art history student's interest in portrait sculpture and her own experience of modelling heads mean that she can comment knowledgeably on the technical skills required to produce some of the artworks she sees in Florence, while the student of Chinese archaeology is able to see the descendants of cookers found in Han dynasty tombs in the cauldrons used in the cafeteria of a modern ferry.

One of the most interesting things about the two accounts is that both writers found something more than the arte-facts they had expected to see: the art history student in Florence found that the paintings she saw evoked not only an aesthetic response in her but also a spiritual one, and a special epiphany in the moment when she felt that she suddenly knew who she was; the student in China, after weeks of difficulties and obstruction as well as opportunities to see marvellous places and archaeological finds, also experienced one of those moments 'when absolute peace descends, moments when the journey is suspended in time.' It is perhaps because of the possibility of such moments, as well as the chance to climb this mountain or visit that museum, that some people travel.

Room Without a View

BETTY LANE

It was late spring. The energy and drive that had taken me through my day job and the Llanover Hall year of ceramics, life-drawing and sculpture was flagging. Llanover Hall is our local community arts centre; soon the centre would be closed except for summer workshops, and Cardiff would become a desert of hot pavements.

Somewhere there was a world out there: India, Africa, Spain, Greece . . . The mind boggles – one can go almost anywhere for a precious fortnight. I had sampled a few places; now it was time to stop and ask myself, 'Who am I? What do I care about? Where will I find it?' As with prayer an answer will be forthcoming, but it is never in the form of a voice you can hear, or a plane ticket dropped from the skies. In my case the answer came in a small advertisement in a Sunday newspaper – *Courses in Art History and Culture, British Institute in Florence* – and an address to write to for information. In the course of time I received their prospectus; as well as providing Italian-language tuition to A-level and beyond, and courses in Italian Opera and Cookery, it offered Italian Villas and Gardens, and Art in Florence. I booked for this last course, at the last moment as always, in a flurry of faxes and passports.

I managed to miss out on booking a room in a street called Via Inferno because I didn't confirm it in time; I still wonder what it would have been like. The one I was offered instead was disappointing. I pressed the bell, the gate opened, and I looked up a tatty staircase – no Roman balustrade, no plush carpets, just stone and concrete. It seemed expensive enough, but Italian money has a lot of noughts on the end and it takes time to adjust to it. My room had window shutters that opened onto nothing: it was a Room Without A View. In the morning I had to look up into a narrow opening to check the small patch of sky at the top for the weather.

There was no time to change; I checked the course time-table I had been sent and found I had just enough time to collect a map and a cappuccino and then find my way to the Institute. As a rule I am hopeless at finding my way around new places, but in Florence I found I could manage; it's a human-sized town, with narrow cobbled streets that reminded me of St.Ives. On the way into the city from the airport I had felt oppressed by the numbers of mopeds and scooters that buzzed like angry wasps through the stradas and across the pontes and piazzas of Florence, seldom giving way to pedestrians. Their presence in such numbers is a result of the ban on motorised four-wheeled traffic in the city centre but in the historic heart of the city even bikes are forbidden, so it was possible to follow the map in peace across the Piazza della Signoria, past the statue of David and alongside the Uffizi museum, conscious that I was passing the home of the gods themselves. I turned right, and there before me was the river. I realised then that my room was in the centre of everything, and I forgave it all its shortcomings and began to love it. There were the fabulous bridges, one behind the other, over the river Arno; I walked past the shops and the Ponte Vecchio, turned left to cross Ponte Trinitas to the other side of the river and then up to the Palazzo Lanfredini, the home of the Institute. From the brilliant sunshine I entered a dark portico and walked through a gloomy vaulted hall: the sun had been shut out, and everything was silent and forbidding. I went up the staircase, and had finally arrived. We were to meet the tutors and the other people on the course, and hear about the goodies in store for us.

The British Institute in Florence is one of the oldest cultural institutions of its type to be established outside Britain, and has been active in the city for more than seventy-five years; its purpose is to promote Italian as well as British culture, and it does this by teaching English to the Italians and Italian to the British. It has a large library in both languages and runs a variety of courses on art, Renaissance history, opera, Italian literature and cookery. The library is fabulous; it holds early editions of D. H. Lawrence, the Sitwells, Virginia Woolf, and others among the angels.

I assembled with other course members at the given time in a room in the library. We sat in rows on chairs crammed in front of a grand piano. We did not introduce ourselves; perhaps that is something only Welsh people do? We would find out about each other, I supposed, by osmosis. We were to meet each morning at a chosen venue with our tutor and the guide for that particular tour, starting with the Bargello; in the early evening we were to return to the library for a lecture. That first evening there was the opening of an art exhibition in an adjoining study-room and here, over drinks with lots of wine flowing, we were able to meet each other.

Later I remember walking back along the river in the dusk, in close conversation with a beautiful young man from Holland. We parted at the Ponte Vecchio because, as fate would have it, he was staying on one side and I on the other. My first day in Florence, and already I was in love! We had time to observe the last rays of the sun halo the clouds and buildings on either side of the river, to be reflected in muted colours in the ripples of water that flowed under the bridge. I could not help remembering that the hallowed ground we were treading on was where Dante first saw Beatrice.

Sunday was a day to remember: the weather was perfect. I had heard someone say, 'Be at Marco via del Servi at 4 p.m. and there'll be a pilgrimage to the Duomo.' I had found out that the Duomo was the cathedral of Florence and that its dome had been designed by Brunelleschi, who solved the technical problem of building such a vast dome by resting the exterior structure on a smaller interior supola. It was an anniversary, although I didn't find out of what. In front of the Duomo the piazza was set out with trestles like any home fair. Crafts and religious mementos were laid out on some while others – and these tempted me more – offered delectable-looking cakes and savouries, with red wine, white wine, and wine of indeterminate colour in bottles, jugs and glasses. I was very thirsty.

But the Elders were gathering at the entrance to the Duomo, gaunt in their dark cassocks; if I stopped to eat and drink now I would lose my place in the procession.

I struggled with temptation for a moment and then, thirst unquenched, joined in behind the priests, the nuns in black, the nuns in white, and the lay people. The distance to the Duomo wasn't great, but the procession moved slowly. Many nuns looked very old. I had seen some fabulous-bodied young Italian women in the city, but here were their older mothers and grandmothers, short and squat, in dark heavy-shouldered suits and pale stockings. From time to time a hymn was initiated by one of the nuns as she walked, and it was then taken up by the long column of people; their voices were strong and sweet but I did not recognise any of the hymns, and I could not understand the words. I had given little thought to the religious beliefs that must underlie them, and I did not know this country or its people. But in a moment of revelation I did know who *I* was: hot, tired, thirsty and alone in a foreign land, perhaps, but I knew I was myself and that I was alive, every part of me, in that place and at that moment.

Our tutor greeted us outside the Bargello the following morning; she was American, which I hadn't expected. After she had sorted out our tickets she informed us in an intense breathy whisper where the toilets were (in the days that followed we found she could always be relied on to make this information a priority); we also learned that much of the best Florentine sculpture still stands in the churches and piazzas for which it was commissioned. The Bargello is a lofty medieval palace, a perfect setting for the heroic sculptures of Donatello, Verrochio, Michelangelo and their contemporaries, including the perceptive portrait sculptures that are my special interest.

And then at last we went to the Uffizi Gallery; I remembered noting, when I took art history exams at Cardiff College years before, that many of the paintings and sculptures I most wanted to see lived in the Uffizi. There seemed to be queues from morning until dusk, but our top person knew their top person and we were ushered past the queues and through a private entrance, which gave us a satisfying sense of having the right connections.

I visited the Science Museum on my own. Here I was especially interested in early drawings of the eclipses of the sun and moon exquisitely drawn on hand-made paper. There were life-sized models of the human womb with a growing baby within it in various stages of development and a special exhibition of the work of Renaissance engineers from Brunelleschi to Leonardo da Vinci, with spectacular working models (I was surprised by the attitude of other members of the group who seemed to think that the

Renaissance relates only to art and literature). My most
memorable visit was to the monastery of San Marco; after
so much elsewhere to please the senses, here was food for
the spirit. Fra Angelico spent a life of prayer decorating his
monastery; in his painting 'The Annunciation' at the head
of the staircase, the clarity of the colours, the tenderness of
feeling and the beauty of the Tuscan landscape in the background were overwhelming. Each small claustrophobic cell
off the long corridor held a painting by Fra Angelico; I
looked up at the poignant paintings of Christ on the Cross
as the monks must have done, and their presence in the
cells where they had lived and prayed was so strong I
could hardly breathe. I walked away from the unbearable
pain of imagining so many crucifixions feeling drained and
weak. We are all different; later, in the gift-shop, I heard
others say that they couldn't take any more madonnas.

At the beginning of the course those of us who wished to
do so were invited to prepare a paper on the subject of our
choice and give a talk to the others. My special interest is
portrait sculpture, and my biggest problem in getting a
likeness is modelling the eyes correctly, because of course
whereas the features of the head are modelled in three
dimensions the eyes are shaped by colour, so this seemed a
good opportunity for research. I explored the library in the
Institute basement, and found many wonderful and out-of-
print books to refer to. Most afternoons, the pull of the
shops or the urge to go to the Boboli Gardens to sip iced
Campari under a striped umbrella was strong, and then
later there were evening meals in the Piazza della Signoria
outside the Uffizi, so I borrowed the books to work on until
late with a bottle of wine in the comfort and seclusion of
my Room Without A View.

We all got to know each other better. One couple seemed
particularly interesting; over drinks and pizzas I found out

that he was doing post-doctoral work in social history at Oxford. She was always quietly and elegantly turned out even when it was hot; he had a wardrobe of interesting and colourful clothes that included bow-ties and waistcoats worn over collarless shirts.

The last day of the course arrived; it was time to give our talks. Mine was well received; there had been a vast amount of appraisal and criticism of the masters by historians and academics, but none of them was in a position to appreciate the technical and practical difficulties of carving stone and marble, of modelling and casting in bronze or hollowing and firing in terracotta, still less the problems confronting a sculptor in modelling the eyes. I especially remember the talk given by one of the A-level students; she was tall and slim, with a pale undecorated face and a fall of shiny uncut hair, and her subject was Fra Angelico of San Marco. She managed to put into words the 'ineffable glow of the spirit' that his paintings had evoked in her, and we were able to experience this again through the slides that accompanied her talk. I awaited the presentation of the Oxford social historian with interest (I knew that he too had worked late) but he didn't appear, and said afterwards that his work 'wasn't good enough, so I decided not to read it'. For me, being over-critical takes away the fun – and besides, it *was* a holiday.

When I got home I found that a new kitten had arrived and needed a name. She is noisy, beautiful, full of life and ready for new experiences, and I called her Florence.

On and Off the Wall

CARMEN LANGE

In 1990, while taking a Master's degree in Chinese archaeology, I felt I needed to see the country and try to understand something of the culture which had produced what I was studying, so decided to use my student loan to spend six weeks backpacking through China.

In Beijing it seemed at one point as if I would be the only visitor not to see the Great Wall, for the Chinese Tourist Information Office CITS (which I promptly renamed ZITS on the grounds it was a blot on the landscape) refused to help: I had come on the wrong day, their own tour ran only on Tuesdays and Thursdays, and I would have to accommodate myself to this. But I was leaving that evening and would not be in Beijing on a Tuesday or Thursday, I protested. The reply was a shrug. When I asked about local buses or taxis, the tourist information officer literally turned his back and ignored me until I left the office; I learned afterwards I should have bribed him, but in fact any bribe would only have produced the same (lack of) information, this time with a smile.

Eventually the assistant at my accommodation hall at the University of Beijing told me about the daily tour for locals and we went together on this; she acted as interpreter and guide and I paid for everything. Every time the bus stopped an extra sum was demanded over and above the initial charge, until all the other passengers were commiserating

36

with me on having to deal with this on a daily basis. On reaching the Great Wall I realised we would be taken round yet another uninteresting exhibition of foreign money and the greatness of the Communist Party, so I dragged my guide directly to the Wall. You would have thought I had threatened her with death by a thousand cuts, so fearful was she of breaking the rules. It is often argued that the Wall was built in order to keep out the pasturalist Mongolians, but the presence of gates set into it at intervals gives lie to this story; the gates were for trading, and great caravans met here from both sides of the Wall to exchange silks for jade and ceramics.

From Beijing I travelled overnight on a ten-hour train journey to Datong, a coal-mining settlement (coal was first used as a fuel in China, and the process introduced to Europe by Marco Polo). Coal-dust, I found, was everywhere. By the time my bus reached the Buddhist caves I had come to see, dust permeated every garment, and my face had great owl-like marks where my glasses shielded my eyes.

The Datonese seemed resigned to the great slag-heaps, permanently grey clothing and dust everywhere. This was how they lived, and it brought them work and wealth. The living conditions were as bad as any nineteenth-century industrial slum: shacks four metres square housed entire families, and cooking had to be done on a stack of bricks outside the front door. There was also wealth: a vast farmers market sold vegetables, chickens, piglets and snakes which had all been brought from the surrounding countryside precariously balanced on the handlebars or packed high into bike-hauled trailers.

Statues from the Northern Wei dynasty (385-535 After the Common Era) are carved into the hillsides above Datong, guarded by the great Buddhist temples. Even the smallest statues dwarf their visitors, who included many Chinese family groups. Everywhere there seemed to be dragons: carved to guard rooftops and guttering, painted under eaves, and spiralling up and down pillars. Chinese emperors declared they were descended from dragons, and the imperial dragon is always distinguished from all others – river dragons, rain dragons, snow dragons – by having five claws instead of the more plebeian four.

I decided to move on. Naïvely I thought I could stroll to Datong railway station, buy a ticket and get on the next train, but the reality was rather different. In the station people were officially waiting in queues, but in fact queue-jumpers (all of them young men) would leap onto the rails dividing the line of people – even sometimes onto heads and shoulders – to get to the front of the queue and buy a ticket. After struggling in the crowd for over half an hour I finally arrived at the ticket window only for some young punk to try to climb over my head. I turned and snarled Welsh curses at him so ferociously he fell off the barrier. He had the last laugh, however: *ferengi* (foreigners: always said with a sneer) had to queue at another window. Nothing I said or did could alter this, so I meekly joined the new queue only to have the ticket-window slammed shut in my face the moment I reached it. It must be lunch-break time, I thought, only to discover that, as a westerner, I should have bought my ticket from the tourist information office, where I would have been charged four times the standard price.

I finally reached Tai Yuan after another overnight train journey, found a room in a hotel which would take foreigners (the Chinese won't direct you to any others) and set off to explore the Song Dynasty Buddhist temple – from the Northern Song period (960-1127 C.E.) – which is the town's only claim to fame. The wooden temples were guarded by lions and more dragons. Cresting a hill I found myself looking at a vast artificial lake, once a place of contemplation and now covered with small paddle boats, but still with a powerful sense of tranquillity. I drifted through the suburbs. A pair of twin pagodas attracted my attention, and I found their base surrounded by bonsai gardens; the trees were several hundred years old (the Chinese were the first to plant trees in pots and miniaturise them).

I gathered my baggage and took yet another overnight train to Xian, to see the pottery army and the tomb of Qin Shi Huang Ti (from the third century B.C.E.). Nothing in books or on TV had prepared me for the massive size of the excavation site. With their usual practicality the Chinese erected vast pavilions (humidity- and temperature- controlled) over the sites before the first trowel touched the earth. Quin Shi Huang Ti was buried in a replica of the palace he lived in, but one vastly improved – as he saw it – to accommodate the improved and magical conditions of the afterlife. Records tell of a mercury lake on which gold and silver ducks swam. At the time of writing, three armies have been found. Each figurine was individually produced, and it is my belief they were modelled on members of his real-life army. The necessary labour-force would not have been a problem in a slave-owning society.The figurines were made from local earth, which suggests the great lined and roofed pits housing them were made by the extraction of the clay. Against their natural background they are barely visible, almost as if in camouflage. With the soldiers, each with perfectly-detailed armour and hairstyles denoting rank and occupation – archer, groom, and so on – are buried dismantled chariots, great heaps of arrows, and replica bronze horses decorated with granular silver bridles.

Eventually I moved on to Chang-an and the burial finds of Princess Di (pronounced DEE). The museum houses the intact remains of the princess, who was 67 years old, had outlived both her husband and her son, and died – probably from heart failure – shortly after eating melon (forty-seven and a half seeds were found in her stomach and upper intestine). Her husband was buried only three metres deep and her son six metres, but Di had her tomb dug to a depth of nine metres. This created phenomenal anerobic conditions which led to the almost perfect preservation not only of her body but of the tomb contents. Entire sets of laquerware were recovered, including her personal make-up kit and food trays. Her corpse was preserved in a liquid mixture that still baffles scientists, but which allowed such a perfect state of preservation her intact limbs were still supple and a proper autopsy could be carried out. She was buried within three coffins, the outermost draped with a banner depicting the legends of the mushrooms of immortality and the story of the queen who stole the elixir of immortality from her husband and fled to the moon: legends which persist in China to this day.

I travelled from Chang-an to Wuhan, which produced a jewel: the museum of the Marquis of Yi, buried in the third century B.C.E. with forty tonnes of bronze in the form of massive candelabra, a double set of bells each inscribed with the sequence in which they were to be played to produce popular tunes of the time, and other ornaments essential for daily life at court. In a small shop I bought two beautifully-made blocks of ink for my own attempts at Chinese painting. The best ink is made from lamp-soot ground to a fine powder and mixed with glues and resins to create hardness and give sweet scents. To use, it is ground against an ink-stone with a small amount of water, the whole process being one of meditation in which the painter stills the mind in preparation for painting. One painter, of the thirteenth century C.E., is said to have stared at the blank paper in front of him for weeks before discovering the painting within it. He then seized a brush and executed a few sure swift strokes to produce a master-piece revered to the present day. Many of the most respected painters in early China were women.

After two days in the intense heat of Wuhan I boarded the ferry for Shanghai, sharing a cabin with a young mother and her three-year-old son. Southern China was more open to foreigners than the north (the Portuguese were regular traders in southern China from the sixteenth century onwards) and this may be why I attracted far more interest than I had been accustomed to receive in the previous weeks. When queuing in the cafeteria I was instantly singled out by a spry elderly professor who took it upon himself to instruct me in the correct procedure and, when he discovered I am vegetarian, to order me a suitable meal.

The cafeteria itself was very basic, with rough plank tables and simple benches. The great cauldrons, placed in metal racks over briquette-fuelled braziers, were direct descendants of cookers found in Han Dynasty tombs (from the second century B.C.E. to the third century C.E.). Hand-ing me a pair of disposable bamboo chopsticks still joined together at the top, my new friend guided me outside and on to the top deck where most of the other diners had gathered, clearly preferring the open air to the stifling dining room. Seagulls screamed and swooped to catch and devour the leftovers. The professor and I talked until he retired for the night and I was left with just the river and the dark. There are times in my travels when a sense of absolute peace descends: moments when the journey is suspended in time. The Yangtze at night gave me some of those moments.

A few hours later I woke to the port of Shanghai, gleam-ing in the distance like a new world beckoning. In the city the professor appeared as if by magic at my side to point out places of interest and give advice on places to stay (unfortunately his information on how to reach them was totally misleading). Having finally found the Youth Hostel and left my backpack there, I emerged ready to explore the city – only to be pounced on by one of the many touts who lie in wait for tourists.

I found myself on a whirlwind tour of the city, hurled on and off buses with a vigour and speed that left me shell-shocked, and for a long time afterwards was unable to disentangle *this* temple from *that* park. The only objects I remember were vast pieces of jade, one a life-size reclining Buddha in pale green stone intricately laced and decorated with gold, which was brought from Burma in 1882. The only place I remember clearly is a tea-house at the centre of an artificial lake at the heart of the public gardens, the walls filled with glorious caddies and exquisite tea-pots. Here I was not only the only foreigner but also the only woman on the premises, but none of the men took the slightest notice of my presence and for that reason alone I suppose I must thank my guide. One day I will return to Shanghai and spend more time there; I particularly loved the evenings, when everyone dragged chairs into the street and sat talking, drinking tea and cooking until the small hours.

By now I had been travelling non-stop for five weeks, and was in serious need of luxury and space. In Hangzhou I found both, and cosseted myself in a hotel. I mooched around the vast lake for three days, sitting in parks, drinking tea in tiny tea-houses and smiling at the honeymoon couples for which this glorious place is renowned. I took a trip into the hills by cable-car to visit a small tenth-century temple. The cable-car had no doors and was packed with several sacks of cement, which tilted it to an angle of 45 degrees plus. The temple was a ruin but the view spectacular.

On the way back I walked past vast fields of tea where a tea-maker turned the leaves by hand in great copper kettles set over the now familiar briquette fires. The tea was sharp and clean and the air was clear, and I remembered those lazy happy days long after I reached home.

III

CHILDHOOD AND ADOLESCENCE

Unlike the writers of many other pieces in this book, the writers of the three pieces in this chapter had no choice as to where they lived or for how long: those decisions had been made by their parents and they themselves had no say in the matter, nor in many other factors which would affect crucially not only their experiences as children but the pattern of their future lives. Their relation to Wales is therefore different fom that of many other writers represented here, and there are also considerable differences between the three of them.

The writer who recounts an incident from her childhood in Jamaica had been born in Wales and had lived here for long enough to have very vivid memories of the area where her family had their home, so that she is in a position to use Wales as a reference point and to make direct comparisons between aspects of her life in Wales and in Jamaica. The writer who describes the formative experiences of her adolescence in India had been born in Britain and had lived here until the age of six, when her Welsh mother took her to India; she wrote the piece from the perspective of someone who had later lived for many years in Wales but, given the nature of the stratified colonial society she describes, the significant differences in her account are between British and non-British, not between Welsh and non-Welsh. The writer whose early life was spent in Russia and Ukraine had not only residence but very close family connections to the country she lived in through her mother and her beloved grandparents; her knowledge and experience of Wales, and therefore her ability to use it as a point of comparison for her early experiences, came later.

These pieces are written by adults remembering events of their childhood and adolescence rather than trying to describe those events through a child's eyes, but their memories still reflect something of a child's view of the world. They give vivid accounts of the houses and gardens they lived in, the colours of clothes and walls and the natural world around them, and they include particularly a vivid recreation of the smell and taste of delicious food. The pleasure they felt in these things helps to give an immediacy and sense of delight even when the events in the foreground (in the accounts from Russia and India) are cruel, violent or tragic: Civil War, attacks by bandits, hunger, political purges and disappearances, parental cruelty and the loss of the one true love.

Against hardship and difficulties such as these, the account from Jamaica perhaps helps to redress the balance; although it deals only with one incident, it offers the possibility of warmth, kindness and companionship between a girl and a woman of different generations, social classes and races. It is easy to imagine why the writers of the pieces set in Russia and India would have such clear memories of the dramatic and often painful events which they describe; it is equally easy to see why the Welshwoman writing of her Jamaican childhood would value the friendship shown to her and remember so vividly some moments of happiness.

Growing Up in Russia and Ukraine

HELEN WAREING

I was born in Ukraine in July 1914 in the small town of Yuzovka, whch had been founded by John Hughes, an ironmaster from Merthyr, in 1869. He was joined by a group of British engineers and skilled workers who included my paternal grandfather. Most of them were bachelors and some of them married there; my grandfather married a Polish woman. My mother, a Russian girl, met my father (who although born in Russia was a British subject) at a dance at the Yuzovka British Club. My mother's parents were reluctant to agree to her marrying Willie Clark who was thought to be wild and irresponsible, and there was also opposition to the marriage from his widowed Roman Catholic mother, who taunted him bitterly for marrying a member of the Russian Orthodox Church.

My maternal grandmother was of German origin, her mother having travelled to Russia in the middle of the nineteenth century to be a governess in a Russian family; on her way she met a young German man who was also travelling to Russia, and married him. They never returned to Germany, but she died at the age of ninety-two still unable to speak Russian properly.

My maternal grandparents lived in a large bungalow just outside the village. It was built of brick, was whitewashed outside and inside, and had a red iron roof; it looked very

47

attractive. There was a small meadow in front of the house, and a cherry and plum orchard at one side with a high stone wall which separated the grounds from the main street of the village. At the back was a large yard with several outbuildings: a lavatory, a chicken house, a cow shed and a cellar. There was also an underground ice-house, filled every spring with large blocks of ice and partly-solidified snow, and used as a refrigerator. In the middle of the yard was a large brick stove, sheltered from the sun by a large roof supported by four posts and open at the sides, on which my grandmother did all the cooking in summer, moving to the indoor kitchen when the weather began to get cold.

Shortages of food were terrible, and thousands of people died of starvation. Sometimes I went with my aunt Sonia to collect our bread ration and I remember seeing people sitting or lying at the roadside with their hands stretched towards us, begging for bread; they were grey-faced and emaciated and could hardly move. The bread ration was very small, but it is an indication of the kindness in the Russian character that the shop assistants who weighed it out always cut the bread just under the correct weight of the ration, and then added a small slice to make up the correct amount; it was understood that the small slice would be given to beggars, and it almost always was.

We never had enough food, but we were luckier than town-dwellers: we had a large garden with fruit trees where we could also grow vegetables and grandmother kept a cow and some chickens, but we did not see sugar, tea, flour or meat for weeks. My grandmother made and remade our clothes, concocted coffee out of roasted acorns and tea out of dried-up grated carrots, looked after the poultry and also managed to find something to give the numerous beggars who came to the door. During the years of the Civil War money lost its value almost as soon as it was minted. By the end of the war, my mother, an accountant, was paid several millions of roubles a month which bought almost nothing, but occasionally part of her salary was paid in kind: a bag of coal, a few pounds of flour, or some potatoes.

Of course, as a child I did not know the full extent of the hardships my family had to endure. My grandmother had a nephew called George who occasionally stayed at our house for a few days. One day, when I must have been five or six, he came in with a stray puppy he had found somewhere; I went out to see it and gave it a crust from the slice of bread I was eating. My aunt Sonia called me from the house and asked me where I had been. When I told her I had just gone to give a crust of bread to Uncle George's puppy, she said 'Why didn't you give it to me ? I'm so hungry.' I was shattered with guilt and burst out crying. Of course I had known there were shortages of food, but as I myself never went hungry I did not realise how desperately hungry my aunt, a growing teenager, must have been.

One day, when I was coming home from school one of the bigger boys in the class, obviously repeating something he had heard from an adult, said 'Your grandfather is a bourgeois.' This was the most insulting word anyone could use, and I hit him. He was so furious that he knocked me into the snow and would have beaten me black and blue if a peasant woman who was passing had not intervened.

During the Civil War our village and the town of Yuzovka changed hands at least a dozen times, the Whites and the Reds each staying for a few weeks before being driven out by the others. Whichever was in control of the district, we almost always had to billet some of the officers. As far as I remember they were all courteous, brought their own rations, and did not take anything away; it was not their fault that they were crawling with lice which they left behind them. Several times our village was attacked by bandits, deserters from both armies. The most notorious band was led by a crazy man called Makno, and nothing was safe from them; they took everything they wanted and shot anyone who protested. On one of these 'visits' to our house the bandits demanded food, and when our servant told them we had none and asked them to go, one of them pushed her against the wall of the kitchen, pulled out his gun, called her all sorts of names for protecting her bourgeois employers, and threatened to shoot her if she did not produce some food. I was in the doorway paralysed with terror, watching my mother begging them to take everything they wanted but to leave the servant unharmed. Suddenly – for no reason I could see – they vanished as quickly as they had come.

When I was nine years old the village council wanted to start a club for the villagers and for the workers in the mines and the small local engineering works, but had no suitable building; grandfather received a notice to leave his house within a week. He was unable to find us anywhere else to live in time, and all our furniture was taken out of the house and dumped in the yard; only the little back room where our servant slept was left for the whole family. It was the middle of winter and bitterly cold, with thick snow on the ground. During the night grandfather and the uncles took turns to walk outside and guard the furniture, while the rest of the family huddled in the little back room trying to get some sleep. This lasted for a few days, during which some of our belongings were stolen and the grand piano cracked with frost and had to be abandoned. Finally Uncle Constantine managed to get us a permit to move into one of the rooms of a flat which had been part of a landowner's house.

One day in April 1925, when I was walking along the top of the stone wall surrounding the house, I saw a well-dressed man in a *hat* (I'd never seen a man wearing such a hat), with a large black moustache and carrying two big brown leather suitcases, getting down from a horse-drawn cart a few yards away and walking towards our gate. I literally rolled off the wall, rushed into the house and, shrieking 'Mother, Mother, Father's come!', hid myself under the bed. Shortly afterwards I was dragged out by my grandmother and with great difficulty persuaded to appear in front of my stranger father.

Later in 1925 the Soviet government started extensive schemes for the electrification of the country; my father was working for the Manchester firm Metropolitan Vickers Electrical Company, which signed a contract with the USSR to supply their power stations with electrical equipment and to provide engineers and fitters to install this machinery. My father had been assigned to work on the Shterovka Power Station in Ukraine, and he had come to Yuzovka to collect my mother and myself before starting his job there. So my mother and I left my grandparents and the village near Yuzovka and the house with the red iron roof at the side of the cherry orchard, and moved to Novo-Paulovka, the village where the power station was to be built. It was very picturesque, with white-washed thatched-roofed houses and orchards behind them. We stayed for a few days in a hostel for foreign workers and then found lodgings in one of the peasant houses; we had one room, their parlour, and they moved into their only other room, a large kitchen. It was not an ideal place since our windows looked on to the market square, which was noisy and smelly and had a slaughter-house at one end; as soon as the weather began to get warmer, our room was filled with thousands of flies. Fortunately we only stayed there for a few weeks before moving to a small two-roomed cottage which stood a little apart from the village and had a large piece of ground in front of it and a stream running alongside. I was eleven years old and had never attended a real school as there had been no suitable schools within reach of the village where I had lived with my grandparents but I had studied regularly with my Aunt Sonia, following the official school syllabus as by then education for children had become compulsory.

The decree to 'liquidate' illiteracy had been signed by Lenin in December 1919 while the Civil War was still raging; it stated that the entire population from eight to fifty had to learn to read and write, either in Russian or in the native language of the republic they lived in. When this decree was signed, literacy was estimated at 30% over the Soviet Union as a whole, but in some areas in the north and the Asian republics it was 2%, and some nationalities had no written language. It was an enormous undertaking to provide teachers and school buildings for such a vast and varied population, and even by the late 1920s schools still worked under great difficulties: because there were not enough school buildings schools had to work in shifts, and there were no textbooks, because pre-revolutionary books were regarded as unsuitable and paper- and printing-shortages meant that not enough new ones could be printed. Some books were printed in very limited numbers for teachers only, and the children had to write down at the teacher's dictation all they had to learn on the different subjects; my aunt was lucky enough to get hold of a few textbooks to teach me. The quality of the paper used for these books and for exercise books as well, was terrible, thin and grey; pencils were precious and had to last for months. I was very lucky; at the beginning of the 1917 Revolution, when my grandfather lost his job as manager of a large estate and his office was closed, he brought home stacks of files containing old correspondence, and as it was written or printed on only one side I had a good supply of writing paper. He also had a good stock of pen-nibs and, as it was almost impossible to obtain ink, made his own by boiling elderberries with some chemical; the ink was deep purple when you wrote with it but gradually faded to a faint lavender. Grandfather learned to make all sorts of unobtainable things, such as shoe polish, and when one year we raised a pig and had it slaughtered, he salted and smoked the ham, bacon and sausages, and made shaving brushes from its bristles. These unexpected skills were much admired and envied by those of his friends who remained traditional impractical Russian intellectuals.

At the beginning of the following year, my father was sent to another power station, in Leningrad. The change from the dirty smoky industrial Yuzovka and the small Ukrainian villages I had known to the beautiful city of Leningrad was quite bewildering; until then I had not seen even a large town. When we arrived the city looked shabby after years of neglect, with paint peeling off the walls, the gilt on the church domes tarnished, and road surfaces full of potholes. All labour and resources were assigned to develop heavy industry, and nothing could be spared for building restoration.

We were given rooms in a flat in what had previously been one of the most select streets, sharing it with eight or nine other Metro-Vickers engineers. One of the rooms, which must have been a ballroom before the Revolution, was used as a dormitory for them; although several large crystal chandeliers hung from the ceiling, the room was usually lit by a couple of low-power bulbs. Our family had two rooms, and there was a large kitchen, and also a room where the cook and the maid slept; Mother was asked to act as housekeeper. The engineers must have felt very isolated as they had no contact with Russians except at work, not only because none of them could speak Russian but because social relationships between Russians and foreigners were discouraged.

Towards the end of the summer Aunt Sonia took me to sit an entrance exam to one of the State schools; it was held at the Smolny Institute (the school for Noble Maidens before the Revolution and the seat of the Soviet Government during the first months after it). There must have been hundreds of teachers in the building that day, as each child had an examiner to itself. I was tested by an elderly little woman in reading, given some dictation and sums to do, and asked a few questions about geography; then she wanted to know where I had gone to school before coming to Leningrad, to which I told her that I had never attended school, but had been taught at home. She said I had passed and could enter the fourth class of the seven-year school, took me back to Aunt Sonia and congratulated her on her teaching. We did not tell her that Sonia herself was largely self-taught, as her boarding school had been closed down at the beginning of the 1917 revolution.

I was lucky to be in Leningrad for my first school – it was an excellent one, staffed by dedicated and experienced teachers who had been trained before the Revolution, who now not only had the difficult job of coping with children from vastly different backgrounds and abilities but also had to adapt their teaching to the new methods of the 1920s, which involved free expression. By the time I reached my last two years at school, however, formal training and strict discipline had been brought back, and a rigid national curriculum imposed.

In October of that year my sister was born. Father and Mother became completely absorbed by her and I was relegated to the care of Aunt Sonia, but at the end of our year in Leningrad she went home and soon got married. I missed her terribly and became very self-contained and withdrawn, feeling that nobody cared for me. Father was a very kind man but he came back to Russia too late for me to form a real attachment to him, and I never learned to love and respect him as I did my grandfather.

After the hardships of my early years during the Civil War life in Leningrad was quite easy, with plenty of food and consumer goods in the shops and a market where peasants sold home-produced food. The market was interesting, but also sad: as well as the peasants selling food, there were pathetic old ladies from the aristocracy or professional classes trying to sell their remaining posses-sions to buy food. The only things I coveted were books, and Mother bought me some; my favourites were *Little Women* and *Little Men* by Louisa M. Alcott in a Russian translation. Towards the end of that summer Father was moved to Baku, the capital of Azerbaijan and at that time the centre of the oil industry. It took us three days to get there by train from Leningrad.

I was fascinated by Baku; it was unlike anything I had ever seen before. There were quaint flat-roofed houses in the old part of the city and mosques with brilliant multi-coloured domes and tall minarets; there were dark-skinned Caucasians, many of the men wearing their national costume of fur-lined capes and fur hats (even in summer), with silver-handled weapons hanging from their belts, followed by their veiled women; there were colourful noisy markets, with grapes, oranges, pomegranates, dates, figs and melons; there were donkeys, laden with baskets of grapes or goat's cheese, coming from their hill villages with their fat drivers sitting on top of their load. I roamed the streets all day, wide-eyed and delighted with everything I saw. But this freedom did not last long; Father enrolled me in school, and I was there for the next three years.

The children were from many nationalities: Russians, Turks, Armenians and Georgians, all very friendly and keen on their studies. Any pupil who found a particular subject difficult was assigned a classmate who was good at that subject and could help them. I, for example, was asked to help my best friend in Russian language and literature, and always needed help in Maths. Throughout my years in Russian schools, the only history we were taught was that which concerned revolutions: in France in 1789, and in Russia in 1905 and (in great detail) in 1917. All the information about this was either dictated to us, or we had to copy it from typewritten notes given to us by the teachers. We also had to learn a long poem by Esenin called 'The Ballad of the 26th', commemorating the execution of twenty-six Commissars by a detachment of British soldiers after the British Army occupied Baku in 1918.

The summers in Baku were unbearably hot, and for the hottest few weeks of my summer holidays my mother took me and my little sister back to Yuzovka to stay with our grandparents. The land around Baku was very arid and fresh water was in short supply, so houses had two mains laid: one to the kitchen for cooking and drinking water (which came from the Caucasian mountains) and one bringing water from the sea for the bathroom and toilet. The school was quite near the sea and occasionally we went swimming, but invariably had to go straight home afterwards to have a bath – there were many oil rigs along the Caspian coast and inevitably there were sometimes spillages, so that the sea usually had an oily film on its surface.

Late in the winter of 1930 I became very ill with double pneumonia. There were no antibiotics then and the only treatment was 'cupping' (drawing blood from the congested area) and aspirins to bring down the temperature. On the night of the crisis, after the doctor's visit, a friend's peasant grandmother came to read 'passing away' prayers over me. I was only semi-conscious, but managed to whisper 'Shut up, I'm not going to die', and then went to sleep. In the morning my temperature was normal again.

When Father knew I was on the way to recovery he went to his next job, near Ivanovo in Central Russia, and the rest of us travelled to join him when I had completely recovered. We left Baku in early April when the weather was getting hot, and arrived in Central Russia to find that it was still winter and the dense forests covered with snow came up to the sides of the railway tracks. The snow began to disappear later in April; first it thawed off the trees, then bare patches began to appear on the ground. I started walking in the forest as soon as I could, but was warned not to go too far because there were wolves about. Some of the men went hunting for them on Sundays.

My most vivid memory of that spring is of looking out of the window one morning, seeing the bare branches of the trees covered with what looked like a greyish-green haze and realising that the leaf buds were beginning to open. Within what seemed like a couple of days the black and miserable-looking forest had become green and beautiful and the ground was covered with early flowers. I understood why Russian writers went into such raptures over the Russian spring; I certainly have no words to describe its beauty. Spring in Britain is beautiful too, but it comes gradually and lasts a long time. Russian spring comes suddenly, is over in a couple of weeks, and is quickly followed by a hot summer.

In early summer Aunt Sonia and her two-year old daughter came to stay, both of them looking like skeletons.

Many food stuffs were strictly rationed and others had
become completely unobtainable, but we had plenty of
food because the Metro-Vickers office in Moscow regularly
sent food parcels to their employees all over Russia. Some
of the food came from Britain, and I can still remember my
first sight of tins of Golden Syrup and packets of porridge
oats.

I was sent back to Yuzovka for my final years at school,
as there was no school within reach of the power station at
Ivanovo. At the end of my final year I received my school
certificate, said goodbye to my grandparents for the last
time, and went to join my parents; by that time my father
was working at yet another power station in Ukraine. I
wanted to go to medical college that autumn, but when
Father consulted the chief engineer in the Metro-Vickers
Moscow office he was advised against it; there would
probably be work in Russia for British engineers for only a
year or two more and there was no point in my continuing
my education in Russia, since the qualifications would be
of no use to me in Britain. He offered to take me into the
company office where I could get useful work experience
which might later help me to get a job in Britain and where
it would also be possible for me to start learning English,
which I had previously been unable to do as no teachers of
English had been available in any of the places we had
lived in. So after spending the summer with my parents I
was put on the train to Moscow and had to abandon my
dreams of becoming a doctor. I was just seventeen.

My salary as a trainee office worker was made partly in
Russian roubles and partly in special roubles which could
be used in shops where food and consumer goods unobtainable in ordinary shops were available for foreign currency. I
lived with relatives of my grandfather, who took me in
partly because I could pay for my board and lodging in

these special roubles with which they could get food which was in desperately short supply in Moscow; they were taking a great risk by allowing me to live with them, as any contact with foreigners was highly dangerous. During the two years I spent in Moscow I was unable to make any contacts except the family I lived with and the people at the office.

My first shock on encountering discrimination against and distrust of foreigners came almost immediately on my arrival in Moscow: I went to the Institute of Foreign Languages to enrol in an English class. After filling in a form I had to show my passport (all Russians have to have an internal passport as ID after the age of sixteen), and as soon as I showed the British passport I had received at sixteen, the official took the form from me and without even looking at what I had written on it, said that all the English classes were full; my British passport was enough to close the door to further education. My employers were not surprised and suggested an accountant who worked in the office as my first teacher. She taught me the basics and then passed me on for private tuition to a professor of English at the university who agreed to take me as long as I paid him in the special roubles.

In February 1933 my father finished his work at the power station in Ukraine and took my mother and sister back to England. The chief consulting engineer said that I could go on working in in the office until it closed, which would probably be a few months later. At the beginning of March I was away from the office for several days with a feverish cold and when I returned on March 13th there were no Russian staff left except the cleaner, and just two Englishmen who had recently arrived in the country.

They told me that the three senior British consulting engineers had been arrested on the night of the 11th at their homes and that they did not know what had happened to the Russian staff. They were very relieved to see me and suggested I should stay at the house in the country where the British staff lived. I arranged to go back briefly to my relations in Moscow; I knew that they would be worried sick when they read of the arrests. When I arrived back at the flat, the old lady threw her arms around me and hugged me with tears running down her face.

Three other Metro-Vickers engineers from different power stations were arrested and the entire office staff now consisted (apart from me, a junior typist) of new people who knew no Russian or anything about running an office; things were chaotic. At their trial, four of the arrested Britons were acquitted but had to leave Russia immediately; the other two were imprisoned but released after six months. I never heard what happened to the Russian staff. In July the junior consulting engineer had to return to Britain and he took me with him to join my parents in Surrey.

I was glad to see them, of course, but heart-broken at having to leave Russia. In spite of the hardships I had had a very happy childhood, and my later years at school and work were happy too, with close and affectionate relationships established with friends in the different places I lived in. It took me years to get used to living in England and to the lack of warmth in personal relations there. It was only when I came to live in Wales that I felt this warmth again.

A Jamaican Childhood

DAVENA HOOSON

The house was in darkness. I strolled barefoot over to the edge of the garden and looked across at the coconut walk; the grass was burnt pale and the long dark spikes of coconut leaves moved in the invisible currents of air. Further off were the mountains, black and silent, a solid featureless backdrop, dense with dark trees, night creatures, fruits and orchids, and abundant with possibilities. Overhead, the Milky Way cut a blazing trail across the shimmering sky.

I remembered a similarly winding path, one strewn with cockle shells cracked and crushed under foot, and bordered with rows of plump vegetables and next door's fence, the haunt of marauding cats, a path shaded with pink old-fashioned heavy-headed roses and scattered with dropped clothes-pegs, the path in Wales which led from my grandparents' back door to the far hedge which bordered the farmer's field. In the hedge was a small round hole you could wriggle through into the field beyond. The field itself was cool and green and empty, but its hedgerows were heavy with blackberries, hazelnuts, dog roses and honeysuckle: a field of tall grass, squeaking and clean in spring and whispering and dry at the end of summer, with clover to suck and daisies to thread. Around me the evening air smelled of dry dust, hot stone and sweet perfumed night flowers; above me the stars looked like cockle shells.

'Hello, Carmarthen', I said quietly, and then walked back to the dark house.

*   *   *

On our arrival in Jamaica we had stayed in a guest-house run by a woman from Llansteffan; it was a pleasant co-incidence and I'm sure it helped us to settle in more quickly. She wore halter-neck dresses with floaty multi-layered skirts and her hair was pulled back from her face Spanish-style. Her nails were long and painted a brilliant vermillion. During the hot afternoons at the guest-house I played with the daughter of one of her maids. She was called Fanchita, which was not her real name but one she'd made up. She showed me the wonderful things in a tropical garden, and through her I began to understand the Jamaican patois.

My parents moved us to a house of our own and we had our own maid, Hazel. I liked her immensely, and especially enjoyed being with her when she cooked her one meal of the day, in the evening. She never sent me away, but she wouldn't stand for any nonsense. She wouldn't use our cooker, preferring to cook over a little wood fire in the back yard; her utensils were an oversized spoon, a lethally sharp knife with no handle, a tin plate, and an old dented can with a badly fitting lid which she used as a cooking pot. I thought her food was always better than ours, even though she used almost the same ingredients.

I loved watching the ceremony of her supper: the setting and lighting of the fire; the stirring of the meal cooked in the can, the making of the little johnny cakes which looked and tasted so much better than our dumplings and the way she ate the food from the tin plate with the big old spoon, clearly enjoying every mouthful.

'What are you putting in it tonight, Hazel?' I asked. We were hunkering down beside the can of boiling water containing the red beans which Hazel called peas. She was adding chunks of yam to it, and answered patiently 'Fish, Miss Dove' (To her, 'Davena' was no name for a girl.)

'Where's the fish ? Shall I fetch it?' I asked, always keen to join in the cooking. 'Shall I clean it for you? I don't mind taking the insides out.'

'Miss Dove, I doan want de fish! Rest and stop troublin' me wid all dis question!'

I sat and watched in reverent silence as Hazel started to tear up some callalloo to add to the pot and then added the pale yellow ackees which turned a wonderful bright buttery colour when cooked. She tapped the spoon on the side of the metal pot, rested it on a scrap of newspaper, and tucked her colourful skirt round her legs. She started to hum as she re-did one of her little plaits; it stayed where she left it, sticking up from her shiny scalp. I liked the way Hazel did her hair. It was divided into neat squares, and at the centre of each was a stiff little plait. Hazel's skin was very dark, almost a blue-black colour. Her forehead shone like polished coal, her skin smelt of warmth, her teeth were always gleaming, and her wide nostrils and big lips were a constant source of wonderment to me. I thought Hazel epitomised everything a black woman should be.

'Go fetch me fish, Miss Dove, den you cyan put it in me pot.'

'Gosh, thanks, Hazel!' I jumped up and ran across the porch and into Hazel's room. There beside her single iron bed was a battered old blue chair and a shabby little table. I picked up the parcel on it which was wrapped in the *Daily Gleaner* and carried it outside. Hazel carefully unfolded the paper and laid it open on the ground beside us.

'See? me already tek off de scales and clean it out. Now,

mek sure de fish doan move from dere, Miss Dove, while I
stir de pot', she instructed. She picked up her big spoon
and gave the contents of the pot a good stir, then ladled out
a steaming spoonful of liquid which she carried to her lips
and noisily slurped. 'You wan some?' she asked. I nodded
hungrily and opened my mouth like a young bird waiting
to be fed even before Hazel had put her spoon back into
the pot. She blew on the mixture and tipped it into my
mouth. The hot, spicy mixture burned my tongue a little
but tasted wonderful. I widened my eyes and smacked my
lips and Hazel laughed her deep-throated chuckle.

'All right. You cyan put de fish in, Miss Dove.'

'You haven't cut the head and things off yet,' I said.

'Oh, me doan boddah wid all dat. Put dy dyam fish in,
gyal!' she ordered. 'Mek haste now, man, me stomach
burnin' op.' She sucked her teeth impatiently with a noise
that sounded like an angry cat, so I quickly lowered the
fish into the broth and wiped my fingers on my bent knees,
watching as Hazel pushed the fish down with her spoon.

''Im soon cook now.' She sat back on the concrete step of
the porch and rested her elbows on her shining knees. Her
skirt looked like a hammock between her legs and I teas-
ingly threw a handful of parched grass from the edge of the
lawn into it.

'Stop yer nonsense man!' she scolded, impatiently brush-
ing the grass away. 'Where you bin since school today?'

'We went to watch the polo for a bit,' I replied absently. I
watched as the soup boiled and bubbled. We sat quietly, an
easy stillness between us. There was a new moon in the sky.

'You want some, Miss Dove?' she asked.

'Yes please!' I said. 'I'll get a plate.' I ran through the
back door and into the kitchen, opened the crockery cup-
board and was helping myself when my father's voice
came from the lounge.

'What are you doing, Davena?' he demanded. I could hear the voice of Maria Callas on our new radiogram.

'I'm just getting a plate. Hazel's going to let me have a taste of her supper.'

'Davena, come here!' My father was cross. 'How many times do I have to tell you you do *not* take food from Hazel? It's her main meal of the day and you've only just had your dinner. Put that plate back and don't be so damned greedy and thoughtless!'

I put the plate back and went to stand by the back door, head down and tears pricking my eyes. I felt humiliated.

'Whachya done now?' asked Hazel, her mouth full of fish.

'Daddy says I can't have any because I've already eaten and it's your dinner not mine. I'm sorry, Hazel. I didn't think.' Over the hedge I could see the lights of other bungalows twinkling through the trees. I blinked back tears; it wasn't fair, and I wouldn't have had much. It was the sharing I wanted, not just the eating.

'Come sit wid me, Miss Dove. Come taste de fish now, chile!' I turned to see Hazel, her outstretched arms beckoning to me in the dark, her tiny fire a glowing vermillion cone between her feet, her white teeth gleaming. I walked over to sit beside her and she offered me a spoonful of fish. I could hardly get the big spoon into my mouth but I tilted my head back and let the food fall into my mouth. I returned the spoon to a grinning Hazel and chewed on the moist spicy food, smiling in enjoyment. It was a few seconds before I could speak.

'This is wonderful! Thank you! I love the ackees!'

'You wan more?' offered Hazel.

'I'd better not, thanks, but it's really smashing. I wish we had food like this!'

'You do eat food like dis, Miss Dove, but not all cook in de same pot.'

'No', I insisted. 'It's good, but somehow it's not the same.'

Hazel looked up and smiled at me; seeing that the coast was clear, she passed me another spoonful. From inside the house the voice of Maria Callas rose into the night air and a door closed. I took the spoon from her and raised it to my lips; I could feel my mouth opening in a smile. There was a soft stillness in the air and above us shone the perfect moon.

The Jacaranda Tree

LETITIA MARY DAVIES

We had lived in the small but beautiful south Indian town for just over a year; I had been born in Britain and had been taken to India by my Welsh mother when I was six. There, circumstances had taken her from the security of a comfortable home with servants to the tiny cottage in which we now lived. Behind her lay two broken marriages, with a child from each as a permanent reminder. There were no servants and very little money. It had been traumatic for us too; my sister and I had loved her father, whom we had lost in circumstances we did not fully understand, but my mother did not discuss the past, although her bitterness was very apparent. Our cottage was small and white, with purple, red and orange bouganvillaea on the boundary fence competing with the deep blue of the Morning Glory. From the house you could see the huge all-enveloping jacaranda tree that stood at the crossroads.

My mother was still young and beautiful and had many admirers. She could have remarried and gained financial security, but she avoided all commitments. She was suspicious of all men, and we grew up in an atmosphere of distrust and overprotectiveness. I adored her and glowed with pride when people commented on her beauty and elegance, but between us there was always some kind of barrier. I did everything I could to please her, and her pleasure when I got a good school report more than made up for the fun I missed because I worked so hard.

Sometimes after supper my sister and I would stroll through the park or down the main street of the town. Often we would spend the evening just looking into shop windows at the beautiful jewellery and ornaments of intricately-carved brass or copper, some inlaid with mother-of-pearl, or the carved sandalwood boxes and chests, and delicately-sculpted chess figures in the robes of the Moghul court. Some shops sold only jewel-coloured gold-threaded silk saris with their heavily-embroidered gold and silver borders, worn with such grace and elegance by the rich and fashionable ladies of the town.

I loved the nights. After the heat of the day the cooler evenings intensified the smell of jasmine or the sweeter odours of Queen of the Night or Temple Flowers, and the moon and stars seemed diamond-bright in the clear black skies. The sky was full of stars, and I regularly counted seven – if you counted seven stars for seven nights all your wishes would come true.

At about this time I made a friend. Pauline's father was army, and he had recently been posted to the local garrison. She and I had a great deal in common, and finally I had a friend of whom my mother approved. Gradually I was given more freedom, provided I was with Pauline. Saturday matinées in the local cinema no longer necessitated the presence of my sister, and I suddenly realised that she had acted as my chaperone; how can you get into trouble with a seven-year-old in constant attendance? It was significant that I did not understand what 'getting into trouble' meant; it was a state often referred to but never explained. Eventually Pauline and I worked it out for ourselves with the help of her older sister, and in horror and disgust we vowed that no man would ever get that close to us.

Pauline did more than secure me freedom: she gave me insight into other homes, other families, other lives. They were a very ordinary family; the sisters quarrelled between themselves and they all argued with the father. Pauline's mother was a no-nonsense down-to-earth army wife who had never had a permanent home throughout her married life, but made the best of wherever they were posted.

It was through Pauline's family that I discovered I was not as unattractive as I had believed. Pauline's sister was training to be a hairdresser, and she used us as willing models for her more bizarre creations. It was she who drew attention to my unusual colouring; she would gladly have traded her own fair hair and brown eyes for my black hair and blue eyes. At night when my mother was out, I experimented with the cosmetics I loved to watch her apply when she was going somewhere special. The powder smelt as she did, of crushed petals. It also went straight up my nose and I sneezed till my eyes ran, but I convinced myself that there was potential in the tear-streaked, red-eyed, runny-nosed reflection in her mirror. I enjoyed the freedom of those nights so much that it never occurred to me that I had become my sister's baby-sitter.

It was Founders' Day: a service in the large chapel of the boys' school in the morning, then a cricket match between past and present students, and a dance in the evening. At midnight the dance ended and the magic ceased to work; until the clock struck twelve a girl could be clasped in the arms of a male while the school staff stood looking on and smiling, but heaven help both boy and girl if they repeated the performance the following day.

It was mid-June and the day was warm and sunny. The gold *mohor* trees behind the chapel were ablaze in the sunshine. Occasionally there was the crack of cricket bat on leather, and applause from the spectators. The old boys were bowling and the present boys were winning, and suddenly my eyes were rivetted on the bowler. We were close enough for me to see that no Hollywood star I'd ever dreamed and sighed over had ever looked like *this*. I was mesmerised. When play ended for lunch I watched him cross over to the pavilion, and then had no alternative but to join Pauline and the others as they drifted away home. I didn't even know who he was.

The evening's dance was a disaster. My mother's out-of-fashion dress did nothing for my appearance and even less for my morale. No one asked me to dance. I sat, overcome by misery, and watched him dancing with a tall attractive girl in a red dress, and my heart contracted. I didn't recognise her, and he didn't even see me. Then it was all over. We sang Auld Lang Syne and the School Song and the National Anthem. It was midnight, and the spell was broken. I did not need a glass slipper: Prince Charming had disappeared.

I could not get him out of my mind. I looked for him everywhere but never saw him, and yet I saw him everywhere I looked, in every tall dark stranger.

The higher I advanced in school, the more my education cost. Even second-hand textbooks were expensive, and I had grown out of most of my clothes. My mother received some money each month from my sister's father, but it was only enough for essentials; anything extra threw the delicate balance into chaos. My mother was constantly under stress, or I am sure she would not have lashed out at me with the unkind things that she said before, it seemed, she could prevent them; I felt I was an encumbrance, and once suggested I should leave school and find work, which brought its own angry reaction. Mostly it was verbal but occasionally she hit out with whatever was to hand. I began to dread the holidays.

Whenever I could I escaped to Pauline's home, but I was soon to lose that support. Her father's regiment was at the end of its overseas tour of duty, and it was rumoured they would be posted back to Britain. When the orders finally came Pauline and her family left in a matter of weeks. The regiment had gone.

My mother was offered a part-time job in the administrative office of the school, and when Founders' Day came round again it was possible for me to have a new dress for the dance in the evening. I was seventeen; my mother and I chose a pattern from a magazine and it was translated into a cloud of blue organdie by our *durzie*, sitting cross-legged at his sewing-machine with an iron heated by live coals to smooth the seams. A pair of cheap white pumps dyed to match completed the outfit.

The day followed its accepted pattern. I missed Pauline but had other friends, and once again we stayed to watch the cricket match. I had dreamed of this moment all year and I searched for the tall dark stranger among the white-clad figures on the field, but there was no sign of him. Around me were male and female voices and snatches of conversation. Someone was whistling *Lazy River*. I turned to leave, since there seemed little point in staying, and my heart lurched. He was standing near the pavilion, hands in pockets, whistling as he watched the game in play. I sat down again abruptly; I could not trust my legs.

Still whistling, he walked slowly down the steps of the pavilion. He had not seen me, and I wanted to cry out to him and beg him not to disappear again from my life. He stopped to talk to a girl I knew who was coming towards us; she smiled up at him. Rosemary was not in my class, but we were in the same hockey team and reasonably friendly. By the time she sat down beside me I had regained my composure sufficiently to ask nonchalantly 'Who was that?'

'My cousin Scott. He used to play in the first eleven

when he was at school, but he wasn't picked for the team this year. He's mad at the selectors.' She laughed. Rosemary always laughed. I could have hugged her.

I dressed carefully that evening. Excitement and anticipation gave me a glow I normally lacked and the new dress gave me a confidence I seldom possessed. Suddenly I was inundated with partners and admirers. I barely sat down, but the face I wanted to see and the voice I wanted to hear did not come near me.

He did not ask me to dance nor did he dance himself, but stood to one side talking with a group of men. I saw him watching as I danced by and once he smiled, but I could not be certain whether the smile was for me or for something one of the men had said. Whenever I could, I watched him. He was very tall and lean and very, very handsome. His hair was dark, but it was his eyes that held me – a strange blue-grey that contrasted dramatically with his tanned skin. He had a slow, rather lopsided, smile, and I realised I was hopelessly in love with him.

I had great difficulty in sleeping that night. Somehow I survived until Monday, when I could ask Rosemary about this relative of hers. I knew I would have to wait until hockey practice that evening, but I still rushed back from lunch hoping that I might see her in the school grounds.

There was someone under the jacaranda tree, sitting astride a bicycle, with one foot on the wall. I was so preoccupied that I was almost next to him before I realised who it was and recognised that slow smile. My first instinct was to run, and I probably would have done so if he had not, whether by accident or design, been blocking my path.

'Hello. You're in a dreadful rush. Meeting somebody?'

'Er . . . hello. No, I have to get back to school,' was the best I could do.

'You obviously enjoyed the social on Friday night. I've

never seen so many bees round a honey-pot. I wanted a dance with you but it was hopeless. You had too many admirers.'

He spoke with unaffected warmth, and I cursed myself for my inability to respond in a light-hearted natural way. My tongue was like lead.

'Well, er . . . I have to go now. Goodbye.' I took off as if all the hounds of hell were nipping at my heels.

Once inside the school grounds I stopped and tried to collect myself. He had talked to me and I had been dumb. I crawled through the evening and the next day and the day after that.

Two days later he was there again. This time it was easier; Rosemary was with him and we chatted without restraint. When we left him and crossed over to the school together she told me about him and her family.

Her grandmother and Scott's mother were sisters, and they lived together with Rosemary's mother and seven children (Rosemary was one of four, Scott one of three) in an enormous house. Scott had recently finished college and was looking for a job. Discreetly questioned, Rosemary confirmed that he had no current girl-friend and that a steady relationship which had lasted for a couple of years was over: the girl had found someone else. I marvelled that any woman could casually throw him aside.

Our afternoon meetings under the jacaranda tree became a regular feature, and though they were painfully short we gradually got to know each other and I lost my shyness. If this was courtship, it was a very strange one. I knew only that my heart raced when I saw him and that the days he was not there were bleak and desolate.

I hated deceiving my mother but I knew she would have prevented me from seeing him if she had known. Scott was Anglo-Indian. His father had been in the British Army and his mother was a local girl, herself the product of an Anglo-Indian 'mixed' marriage. It was a common story: their homes and life-styles reflected the British way of life in which they had been raised but in essence they were a community on their own, not accepted by the British and rejected by the Indian population. By some genetic accident Scott was the only member of the entire family to have a dark skin. I did not even think about it – most of the school and half of the staff were Anglo-Indian – but my mother would never accept a relationship between one of her daughters and a man who was not completely British. Scott was not 'white' and did not have a job. Handsome he undoubtedly was and well educated, but eligible he was not.

I met his family; they were all kind to me and I felt at home with them. That I was in love with Scott was blatantly obvious, but I was still not sure of his feelings for me.

Until the picnic. On that day his family made a sort of pilgrimage to a favourite beauty-spot several miles out of town. It took a convoy of cars to take us through the flat, open countryside, the monotony of brown earth broken by the occasional patch of emerald-green rice fields. Women in blue, red and yellow worked in the fields and children played along the roadside, shouting and laughing to us as we passed. We drove through a large village. Dust rose in clouds, heavy with the smells of the streets – of frying oil and spices, jasmine, woodsmoke, Indian cigarettes, incense and dung.

Our destination was a large lake where groves of casurina trees gave shade from the heat of the day. I remember little of the picnic itself – some people played games, some sprawled in the shade of the trees, someone played a guitar and a few voices sang a popular melody. Scott took my hand and led me towards the lake, and in a small grove of casurina trees, hidden from the others, he drew me to him and kissed me. I could feel the beating of his heart. He told me that he loved me, and I poured out my love for him.

By the time the picnic was over everyone knew that I was his girl. Few were surprised, His mother and his aunt did not seem to mind, But his aunt said, 'It's time you told your mother about Scott, child. Everybody else seems to know.'

I nodded dumbly but did not reply. I could not tell her that I wanted to, more than anything else now that I knew my love was returned, but was too afraid.

The wedding of Scott's sister solved everything: although my mother knew none of his family but Rosemary she still received an invitation. At the reception *she* was the one treated like the guest of honour, and Scott hovered around her solicitously until she was completely captivated by his charm and good manners. When it was over he drove us home and invited us to the pictures the following evening; my mother responded by inviting him to have a meal with us first. She was no fool, and it wasn't long before the situation was clear to her. We never had to meet in secret again.

He must truly have loved me. He was twenty-four and I was a schoolgirl in every sense of the word. We met under the strictest supervision – when my mother was not present my sister was – and yet he never complained. With my family he was friendly and charming and easy. My sister adored him, and gradually my mother began to remove herself from constant supervision; she grew fond of Scott, but never lost her reservations. She accepted the situation because, I think, she believed that the affair would burn itself out sooner or later, and probably sooner if she offered no opposition. The question of marriage could not arise while I was still at school.

The final examination and the end of my schooldays were only weeks away when, in mid-morning, the whole school was summoned to assembly and informed by our grim-faced headmistress that Britain and Germany were at war. My first thought, selfishly, was of Scott: would he be involved in what was happening on the other side of the world?

The examination lasted a week, with two papers a day. The standard was very high and I was convinced at the end of each day that I had failed. I was tired and depressed and cried for no reason. Rosemary had ruined my peace of mind by telling me that Scott's ex-fiancée had come back. I would have liked to become a teacher, but we had no money to keep me for the years of training. My mother decided I should enrol in a secretarial college, and managed to get me some cash from an obscure scholarship fund to pay for it.

We moved from our cottage at the bottom of the hill to a larger house at the other end of the cantonment, and I was no longer be able to see the jacaranda tree. I was unhappy at the move, and felt a stab of superstitious fear at moving so far from the tree which had seen the beginning and blooming of my love. Scott still had no job and my mother made it clear that she would not give her consent to my marrying him; I would have to wait until I was twenty-one and legally an adult.

My ex-stepfather wrote to us to introduce the son of a friend of his, a young reporter who would soon be visiting our town; he arrived almost as fast as the letter. My mother made him welcome and arranged for him to take me out to dinner. Scott was away at yet another job interview and would not be back until late that evening. He would come straight from the station to find me out with another man.

My mother and I quarrelled bitterly, but she was obdurate.

This man was a family friend and I would observe the courtesies; that was an order.

His name was Alan. He was charming, goodlooking, affluent with a promising career, and white. He was sophisticated enough to cover the awkward moments with small talk, but I was not sophisticated enough to pretend. The evening ended early, and he refused an invitation to come in for a drink. I never heard from him again.

I raced into the house, but Scott had already left. He did not meet me after class the next morning, and was not at his home. No one seemed to know where he was.

My mother countered my tearful outburst with a fury that terrified me. Alan was the type of man I should choose; I was wasting my time and my life. Scott was standing in my way; once again he had not managed to get a job. How did we plan to live? Had I no pride? Had I no shame? If *I* was prepared to have a brood of half-caste children, *she* wanted no part of them or me. It was all finally said. Everything I had suspected was true. I hated my mother that day.

He stayed away for two days. He was deeply hurt because he could not understand why I had allowed the situation to develop. If my mother forbade me to see him, he asked, would I obey her as readily as I had agreed to go out with Alan? I despised myself for my inability to stand up to my mother, and if I could have left home I would have done so.

On my way to do an errand for my mother I saw Scott and his ex-fiancée; they were sitting in a coffee-bar which we often visited. If he had been with anyone but her I would have jumped off my bicycle and joined them; as it was, I stopped and then cycled on. Two weeks later I saw them again. They were standing under the jacaranda tree, deep in conversation. He had his back to the road and did not see me but she did, and I knew instinctively that she wanted him back.

I locked myself in my room and refused to talk to him. I tore up all his letters. I made myself ill, and my mother called in a doctor; he prescribed tablets which made me sleep for hours. I went with my mother to stay in the Nilgiri Hills to recover. I realised gradually that I loved him desperately and wanted his love and forgiveness for the way I had behaved, and wrote to tell him so.

There was no time for a reply because we would be home in a few days. When we got back I rushed to his house, but he was gone. He had enlisted in the army and was in a training camp somewhere in the south of India. His mother had re-addressed my letter.

I wrote dozens of letters to him, but had no reply. I prayed for a miracle.

Some months later Rosemary told me what had happened. When Scott had enlisted he came to see me to say goodbye, to try to end the rift between us and to beg my mother to agree to our writing to each other while he was away. He found an empty house. No one could tell him where we were.

So he turned to the woman who had watched and waited. While I was walking the peaceful slopes of the Nilgiri Hills their first child was conceived. The letter I had written followed him from one address to another, and by the time he received it he knew of her pregnancy. So they were married.

I saw him once. It was New Year's Eve in Delhi; he was with his wife and I was with my husband. We did not speak, but everything was said in the long searching look between us before we turned back to our 'real' lives. I live now in a different time and a different continent, and many years have passed. I have my life in Wales, my family, and the world I have made for myself. I have never forgotten him.

The jacaranda tree no longer grows at the corner of the two roads. It and its garden have been replaced by high-rise flats. Where have they gone to, I wonder, the scent of its blossom and the beauty of its flowers?

IV

THIS WORKING LIFE

In some ways, working abroad can seem to offer an opportunity to get much closer to another society than other experiences of travel permit; in contrast to the tourist or casual visitor, who may find that the only people they come into contact with are either those catering for the tourist trade or other foreigners, the woman working abroad may work alongside members of the community she is visiting, live among them – queue in the same shops, eat in the same restaurants and get stuck in the same traffic jams – and may therefore be in a position to have a clearer idea of the details of their daily lives, their modes of thought, their priorities, interests and concerns. That, at least, is the theory; in practice this greater physical closeness may accentuate rather than diminish the difference between them, and the four pieces in this chapter exemplify this.

Sometimes, especially in countries where English is the majority language, the distance between the visitor and the host community can seem bridgeable but it is always there, as the pieces here on life in New York and Australia demonstrate. The Welsh woman is newsworthy in Manhattan as a *British* actress-turned-artist, and is very well aware that her popularity is at least partly due to her 'oddness and novelty value', and that if she stayed long enough to stop being clearly different from the people around her she

would be less interesting to them and her work less market-
able. The Welsh woman in Australia fits into the community in which she lives and works because of shared
artistic interests and a similar attitude towards daily life,
but her landlady's boyfriend constantly reminds her that
she is a Pom and the way-out friend regards her Welshness
as enviably exotic. Her final comments on the natural
world around her – which has had an important influence
on her response to the country she is visiting – reflect on
the fact that when two patches of different colour in the sky
intersect they do not blend seamlessly together but create
something new which is different from either source.

In the other two pieces, difficulties in communication –
through the lack, at least initially, of a common language –
mirror the distance between the two Welshwomen and the
communities they are living in. It is probably no coincidence
that the only person whom the au pair becomes in any way
close to is, like her, an outsider from the bourgeois society
in which she is working, not only through social class (he is
a bus driver) but also, as her analysis of the strata of Cannes
society makes clear, as one of the indigenous inhabitants of
the Midi in contrast to the richer incomers from Paris and
other regions of northern France. The university teacher in
Japan in the late 1960s is thrown into a situation in which
she is alien in a linguistic, cultural and social sense as well
as that of her passport, and she has no guidelines which
would help her understand what she should do and should
not do (still less, *why* she should or should not do it); the
apparent physical closeness she experiences by living in a
Japanese home serves to emphasise her difference and
(literal and metaphorical) alienation from the community
around her rather than to offer her any prospect of becoming part of it.

Manhattan Spice

CAROLE MORGAN HOPKIN

Something had always tugged at my Welsh roots from across the Atlantic. Perhaps it was the early influence of my paternal grandfather who had returned to the Swansea valley to publish his own newspaper after running away to Chicago and working on the *Tribune*. I had been to America before on business (not my business, but all paid for – once to New York, once to L.A. and once to Hawaii) and what I'd seen, I'd liked. Now, having been an actress for seven years and just out of a year in *The Mousetrap*, I felt London's heavy weight pressing on my tiny Shepherds Bush flat. My telephone seemed equally alienated. No calls meant no work, and no work meant boredom and depression. So, hearing that my textile-designer friends were off to New York for a selling trip, my intrepid alter ego decided that I should join them. Standby. Air India.

In the cab from JFK the amazing sight – the tips of Manhattan's peaks rising dark against the glowing technicolour sunset – brought a squeal of delight. 'So you like our city?' asked the friendly cab driver.

My friends sighed. They were used to the place, the people, the tough talking they'd have to do to buyers before the week's end, and very used to my enthusiasm for anything new. After listening to my plans to find a job and a place to live in the little time we had, they both agreed that they'd give me three days to come down to earth. Staring at the

glowing skyline, I promised myself success. I'd have fun,
flirt, learn to speak slower and lower, dress up or down,
wear cocktail hats and an outrageous hand-me-down
ocelot coat, and be able to do it all because I was a complete
stranger, an unknown quantity. What would I find? I didn't
know, but I was sure I'd enjoy finding out.

We three (two successful career girls and me) checked
into a mid-town, mid-priced hotel. Due to my companions'
four years as loyal customers, we were given the perfect
room: three comfortable beds, lots of closet space, and its
own iron and ironing-board – the girls had to look Saks-
smart to impress the buyers.

After a journey of twelve hours we were all knee-
tremblingly tired, but I was determined not to waste a
moment. Consulting my list of events I saw that Monday
was Woody Allen night at Michael's, just a few blocks
uptown. My 'Come on, girls, get your sneakers on' was
greeted with groans; I was on my own.

I seemed to float the ten blocks up and six over to reach
the club at interval time. 'Teeming' wasn't the word, but
the crowd helped support my jet-lagged body as I stood
waiting for the next set. I felt a slight nag of irritation as I
realised the years I'd wasted in London while all this had
been going on here.

When Woody finally played it was pure America. I was
transfixed until the final note. I immediately decided that
the following morning I'd go straight to his office to sell
him my life-story as the plot for his next film. Contracts
would be signed by mid-day and a star would be born.

Bright but not too early the next day I made my way up
Fifth Avenue, but couldn't remember it being so crowded
before. By the time I got to Saks I had to fight my way
through the throng. At St.Patrick's Cathedral I was accosted
by a street-hawker: 'Buy your Pope t-shirt! Don't let the

Pope catch you without one!' So he was in town too, was he? I took it as an excellent omen.

An hour later as I sat, not at all dejected by the lack of enthusiam shown in my life-story by Woody Allen's office, and watching the Plaza fountain raining sundrops I bit into my first Big Apple. Along with a regular coffee-to-go, it was also my first brown-bag lunch. I had arrived!

On my hit-list the BBC was outlined in red, and since I'd worked for them several times at home I decided that they would be my next stop. Half an hour later they joined Woody Allen on my 'rejected' list. Clearly this town would be harder to crack than I'd thought; at this rate, I'd be through by tea-time and free to fly home tomorrow.

'We're only a sales office,' the film-star-lookalike at Reception had drawled. 'Why don't you try the Consulate? They're always looking for clerks.'

A desk job? Me? Hardly, though I daren't admit it aloud. As I made my way over to Third Avenue I thought how much pleasanter this job-hunting was than phone-calls and wasted Tube fares in London, delighting in the city's aromas and colours from the corner stalls of flowers, pumpkins, cinnamon doughnuts and roasting chestnuts.

The British Consulate, however, was exactly as I'd imagined: grey, in its foreboding calm. Even the receptionist seemed a robotic clone of her Westminster sister. My request for work was greeted with a wry smile, and the Personnel Manager herself arrived with a flurry of application forms. All twinset and pearls, she could have been taken for the lady-in-waiting to a Royal. I was offered tea, and as I filled in my details I began to warm to the musty familiarity of Britishness. Playing down my professional acting experience I pushed my administrative skills and my long-forgotten teaching certificate. The Personnel Manager glanced over my c.v., beamed at me, and told me that she thought they would be in touch very soon. I left on a wave of bonhomie.

Drifting back towards the hotel, I thought how pleased my parents would be: their wayward daughter in a proper job at last. A pension, even!

Common sense told me that I should now find a less expensive camp-site. There was one safety-net – relatives back home had friends in Brooklyn, an Italian family who would be happy to put me up. I checked out Brooklyn on my map and saw how detached from Manhattan it was, stretching miles across Long Island.

A phone call got me invited to dinner but as I took the subway, each stop made me increasingly homesick for the city. When I arrived at Fort Hamilton Parkway I walked the twenty minutes to their house with a sinking heart: rows and rows of semis in suburban slumber.

Their welcome, however, overwhelmed me, and after a five-course meal of home-made Neapolitan dishes I felt comfortable enough to forget Manhattan's dazzle. 'Pop' drove me back to Brooklyn Bridge, explaining en route the difficulties of securing any employment in the States without the magic Green Card; if I was lucky enough to be offered work and a Diplomatic Visa I should jump at it with both feet.

And that's what I did. The position offered to me was that of Commercial Assistant in the British Trade Office and, with special responsibility for Fashion and Textiles, not at all as boring as it first sounded. At my interview my boss-to-be asked if I'd noticed much British influence in the stores I'd visited. 'No,' I answered (too smartly). 'I've been quite disappointed, especially in Saks – although it's British-owned I saw even fewer UK labels than in Bloomingdales.' This was not what the four Officers and the 'Royal lady-in-waiting' wished to hear, and there was a gaping hole of silence. The Big Boss coughed and rumbled on about targets, policies, trade shows and receptions I'd have to attend. I perked up my ears at the last of these, visualising caviar on silver platters washed down by liberal glasses of bubbly. Yes, I thought, the job sounded perfect for me. I'd take it.

So I found myself living in Brooklyn and commuting to my twentieth-floor office, with a secretary and a modest expense account. I was handed the British fashion industry on a plate and told to start wooing American buyers and boosting our fuddy-duddy image. My first assignment was handling forty companies due to arrive for the European Fashion Fair. It proved hugely successful, mostly because British hand-made designer knitwear was so popular with Americans that I spent the week just watching our manufacturers taking a healthy stack of orders.

Life was good, very good, and on a visit to Poughkeepsie with my 'foster family' it took another leap forward. I happened to pick up an abandoned *New York Times*, folded at the 'Apartments to Let' section, and read my future: 'Apt. to share. Secure Upper Eastside Bldg. Modest rent.' 'Modest' could mean anything in Manhattan, but one phone call assured me that it was within my tight budget. How could Fifth Avenue be so reasonable?

The answer lay in the age of my landlady. Mrs T. was eighty-eight and 'holding', a sparkling and glamorous lady with two adoring sons who would be happier if there was 'someone here, nights, 'case I fall,' she explained. 'Can you think of such a thing? At my age?' Her laughter tinkled the chandelier droplets, and I knew we'd get along fine. She seemed impressed by my manners, appearance and position at the Consulate just ten blocks away. Without hesitation I accepted a large room with oversized television, private shower-room, share of the elegant reception rooms and maid service, along with the cheery attention of the elevator operator and dutiful doormen.

Despite all 'Mamma's' misgivings about the daily muggings and the general horrors of city life, I moved into Fifth Avenue at the end of the week. My nightlife changed from boarding the 6.15 train to Brooklyn, to sauntering out of my office doors and having Manhattan's partytime ready and waiting for me.

I resisted all the offers to play darts at the British pub on Third, where the Consulate girls congregated, went to only one wine-tasting at the Aussie Trade Office, and politely said no to the staff get-togethers where no one mentioned America but spent the evening consoling each other for what they missed about Britain. Apart from my family I missed nothing, not even digestive biscuits! What I craved were the pumpernickel raisin rolls they served at Nanny Rose on Columbus, coffee at La Bamba, and soda bread from Zabar's.

An enjoyable part of my duties at the Consulate was to act as guide to certain guests. Besides commiserating with the man from Scotland Yard who had to trail behind us when I took the Duchess of Gloucester on a four-hour shopping spree, I advised many British visitors on where to eat the best burgers, buy Blue Mountain coffee, get home-made welshcakes and, in general, savour what New York had to offer. Once, my comments on ex-pat life were quoted in an article in the *Western Mail* which my father came across by accident. Fame at last.

But friends were the reason I stayed so long, and soon a group of us was meeting each evening in a tiny French bistro just off Madison. We were an odd mix, who gathered around a queen bee – an elegant and amusing French lady who had, as a teenager, worked for the Resistance in war-time France. She was a magnet for artists and writers, emigrés from Europe and young hopefuls like me. We'd meet, drink, talk, eat, talk some more, go dancing or to the cinema, a gallery opening, or back to her apartment for a nightcap – it was only five blocks from mine, but much more upmarket. Life sparkled!

Depression was a thing of the past. With the city's energy boosting my immune system to unprecedented heights I went through seven years without a cold, flu, or even a headache. But whereas reading good literature had previously been a daily necessity for me, I had now become a fulltime people-watcher. I observed people and things with a keener eye, tasted, smelt, heard and absorbed each sensation so powerfully that now, ten years on, I can still 'be there' again in an instant. Three years into my stay I realised with a sharp jolt of surprise that since arriving in New York I had not read even one book in any genre. Culture had changed its meaning for me, and was now focused exclusively on people. But then I met a like-minded girl from Manchester and was brought back to my earlier creative aspirations.

She had less money to spend than I did, so we walked everywhere: to church on Sunday for the singing and the after-service coffeehour, to the Guggenheim Museum or the Metropolitan Museum of Art where we'd immerse ourselves in Impressionism and the exquisite Tiffany windows, then a quick hike south to Greenwich Village, SoHo, and a shared bowl of chilli at a sidewalk table on Spring Street. We'd stroll around the galleries and ethnic shops, toast Dylan Thomas in the Cedar Bar with a non-alcoholic drink, and then find a non-yuppy deli to buy bread, cheese and fruit for a teatime picnic in Washington Square. When she joined the library I did too, and when she saw some of my sketches she encouraged me to pick up my paintbrush again. When I submitted a watercolour of Longfellow's home to *Vogue* they promptly featured me as a British actress-turned-painter who would be interested in commissions for house and garden portraits. A gallery in Connecticut phoned to say they'd like to see more of my work. A new world was opening up for me.

Over the next two years I made a name for myself as an artist, with exhibitions in Connecticut, Long Island and Palm Beach. On my solo journeys to Oyster Bay or Cold Spring Harbour I was looked on as quite the eccentric. No one else walked the few miles from the station, no one else sat sketching in the middle of town or on the harbour wall, munching a picnic from Zabar's. My natural curiosity about everything and everyone amused the locals and I was invited to stay overnight by one family after another, many of whom became my patrons. I was fully aware, however, that my popularity was due at least in part to my oddness and novelty value; if I stayed too long I'd be neither new nor interestingly odd.

To leave the Consulate I'd need a Green Card, and the easiest way of getting one was through domestic work. Mrs B. was an ancient millionairess who lived in a double-decker penthouse with two cats. She needed someone to arrange her engagements, write her thank-you notes, take her calls and generally see that she was just ahead of her busy schedule. When I told her about my painting she was delighted. How could I be so pretty *and* so talented? Of course I'd have time to paint when I was working for her, and just think of all the clients she could introduce me to! We were made for each other, and she'd get her lawyers to work on my Green Card right away. I handed in my notice at the Consulate and was given an embarrassingly expensive leaving-present.

Life can take you anywhere you want to go until you get there. My meals were provided, but 'lunch' was half a hard-boiled egg (enough for her, and therefore enough for me) and the fruit-juice carton in the fridge held two inches of juice for me each morning; the rest was safely upstairs in her (locked) kitchen. If she saw more than two bananas on the staff table she'd squawk, 'You eat like vultures – you'll ruin me!' My boyfriend, a lawyer, found out that unless she was so devoted to me that she was prepared to pay $2,000 to process my Green Card quickly, I could have *that* carrot dangling in front of me for years.

I gave in my notice and ran back to the Consulate, where I was told I'd have to wait for an opening. Within two months I was back at the Trade Office, but someone else now had the Fashion portfolio and I was given 'Domestic Appliances' which was not really of much interest to me. I realised that my time in the U.S. was coming to an end.

Ten years on, would I return? Yes and no: yes, for that unique feeling of possibility, the feeling that the best of your life is about to happen. No, because much of what made my time in New York so special has changed – all the people I knew there have moved either to other parts of the United States or back to Europe. The little bistro has closed. Even the Trade Office has been relocated. But I know that, like acting, New York is in my blood and my heart for life, and writing about it is an act of pure nostalgia.

The First Alien

MARIANNE JONES

Four men were waiting for Non at the provincial airport: the head of English and three members of his staff. They fussed her into the university's limousine, which bumped down a dusty road into flat countryside. A glossy orange fruit on a leafless tree against a blue sky – in November – was her first image of Japan.

'Persimmon,' the head of department explained. 'One left for god to give sank for harvest.'

The limousine stopped to let out two of the men, in smart Western suits, so that they could relieve themselves by the side of the road. After this, the car left the trunk road and went down a lane lined with weeping-willow trees to the house where she would be a lodger. It was on the edge of a village near some ricefields and you could see the mountains in the distance. Strings of drying persimmon hung from its eaves.

When they were about to enter the house, the wife of the family got down on her knees and bowed her head to the floor in greeting. From signals too subtle to define, Non sensed it would embarrass them if a guest copied this behaviour and instead smiled awkwardly in the doorway. She was invited to take her shoes off and step into the house, but the head of department was leaving and his staff – including Mr Kumamoto, the head of the house – were going back to work with him. Non was left with Mr Kumamoto's mother and wife.

She felt lost: broken English and embarrassed laughs were replaced by silence. Wondering how they could communicate, she got out photographs of her family and pointed at the people in them. The wife supplied her with words for what must have been 'father', 'mother' and 'sister' and she repeated them and tried to fix them in her memory.

In the evening Mr Kumamoto came home, but he was tired. They ate a silent supper in front of dinosaurs spewing out their guts. This was the favourite TV programme of the six-year-old son who had come home from school, stared at her, and then started drawing cartoon heroes. Mr Kumamoto, in a navy *yukata*, relaxed a little after the meal and did some interpreting for her. She gathered that his mother, called 'grandmother' by the whole family, had been trying to communicate with her during the afternoon by simplifying her Japanese. She had repeated, 'Japan – island. England – island. Japan – king. England – king. Our country – friend. I fan of Royal family and can I have English stamp?' but the only answer she had received was 'father – mother – sister'.

Mr Kumamoto put vinegar in his coffee – to give him strength against the winter, he said. He was reserving moxification and mantrifying 'I feel warm' for later, when it got colder. He translated the question which had been bothering the grandmother all day: 'What are you doing here, Nonna? Shouldn't you be getting married?'

It might cause scandal if she told them about Takeo. 'I want to see the world,' she said.

'You're not scared?' the grandmother asked through Mr Kumamoto. She looked perplexed and asked how people got married in Britain. Her parents had chosen a husband for her early. She had not seen him until her wedding day. 'Then I peep sideways,' Mr Kumamoto translated, 'and I see.'

'Weren't you scared?' Non asked, and they smiled at one another.

The smile reminded Non of her grandparents sitting in front of their coal fire on winter evenings. Their 'young people these days . . . not in my day' remarks burnt like paper in the affection they felt for her and she for them. There was no uncrossable divide between people, not even when there was a language barrier.

'What if he'd been ugly?' Non asked, enjoying the flare of the stove as it was lit and then noticing grandmother's look of shock to her son. Was it so outrageous to refer to what men were like physically? In which case, why had grandmother peeped sideways on her wedding day? 'Or incredibly handsome, of course,' she added politely.

'I learn to love him later.' Grandmother's last sentence was translated as she blew her nose on the sleeve of her kimono.

'Nowadays you see each other first,' Mr Kumamoto added with a grin.

'What would you do if your parents arranged an interview for you to meet suitable young man?' grandmother wanted to know. 'Isn't it a good idea at your age?'

'I'd be cross with them,' she answered.

Grandmother hissed disapprovingly, didn't speak to her for several minutes and sucked down a cup of green tea.

At breakfast the next day, the sides of the house – wooden sections on runners – were pushed open because it was warm. Non knelt on her flat cushion trying to enjoy bean soup with seaweed; it tasted medicinal. She contemplated the raw egg in a laquer bowl but felt that it was too early in the morning to adapt to her new life. The TV was on and grandmother's eyes were full of tears. A young man in uniform was giving a fervent speech to his community before leaving home for the war. His eyes were raised to the flag of the Rising Sun. 'Banzai!' he yelled. Here she was, twenty-five years after these events, eating breakfast on a sunny morning with 'the enemy' and feeling sympathy for the tears in grandmother's eyes. What had happened to her husband?

Going to work on the back of Mr Kumamoto's scooter, swinging round corners, rattling along miles of country roads, was the best part of her first day. Her spirit rode high on sun in winter. As they reached the university city, Mr Kumamoto shouted something to her about the castle moat containing lotus. The roots were harvested and they could have some for supper that week. Non wondered if she would then forget her home and become part of this new country.

That evening, however, Mr Kumamoto had to tell her that his wife was not happy about him giving a young woman like her a ride on the back of his scooter and please could she find her way to work by bus in future. He laughed awkwardly. They were not worried but they feared gossip. She had to understand that.

Over the next few weeks the images of the persimmon tree and the ride on the bike were replaced by those of eyes staring and strangers following her in the street shouting 'Foreigner!' Feeling lonely, she went for long walks along the banks of the willow-lined river. She saw women stitching quilts at the open sides of their houses, and stared across the ricefields at the mountains.

Mr Kumamoto had to warn her that people found her peculiar because she went for long walks by herself. They could see that there was no purpose to her walks; she was not shopping or going to the bus-stop. Non found this hard. She was used to walking in the mountains or down to the beach: fresh air at the end of the day, a chance to be alone with her thoughts. If only Takeo were nearer.

She did not mention problems of loneliness in her letters to him; the winter break was coming and it would cure everything. He was flying down to see her then. She knotted all her strength together and waited. At least she was learning some Japanese.

One morning she received a small parcel and recognised the italic writing of her best friend at home. She tore off the stamps, gave them to grandmother, and ripped open the parcel. It contained a letter and a 'Silver Fountain' firework to celebrate her arrival on Japanese soil. She saved it so that she could light it with Takeo.

Then suddenly he was there, commenting on the mildness of the weather. It was snowing in Tokyo.

The Kumamotos were impressed by being called upon by a scholar from the great city, by the perfection of his manners and his obvious intelligence and learning. They asked his opinion, bowed, and nodded their assent.

Non walked along the river bank with him and he translated ancient poetry for her: poems about princesses gazing out into the darkness at the moon and waiting for the lover from whom they had been parted, or about life floating like leaves on a river and vanishing like a deer into the forest. She remembered the firework – if life was going to be fleeting, let it be full of sparks!

'What firework?' he asked with concern. 'They're very dangerous. We must get rid of it.'

In the end he agreed that he would not stop her lighting it and she agreed to do it at once and not wait for the night. After the silver sparks fizzled out, he apologised to the Kumamotos for their strange behaviour. Naturally, they would not normally light fireworks like this.

'We have firework,' said grandmother. 'in summer, of course.'

'We have them in winter, ' Non said.

Grandmother smiled. 'Not cold?' she asked.

'Very cold! You need a scarf in bright colours to keep you warm.'

They went for more walks in the slightly chill air. Then, as suddenly as he had come, Takeo was gone. It would be spring before she had another break and enough money to visit him.

After he left, as she was sitting alone in her room trying to hold onto the warmth of being near him, there was shouting at the front entrance. She heard Mr Kumamoto's reasonable voice, followed by the raised voices of two or three men and then quiet Mrs Kumamoto shouting hysterically. She was out of her room before she realised she could not help. One of the three men stared at her; another nodded brusquely. Raised voices broke out again. The word 'foreigner' was repeated. Mr Kumamoto's soothing remarks were interrupted. Grandmother looked at her in obvious distress, said something to Mrs Kumamoto and they both retreated into the living room. There was an awkward silence. One of the three men softened, smiled at her and said something to his companions. The one who had nodded brusquely protested but gradually calmed down and the three bowed deeply and left.

Mr Kumamoto explained that this delegation from the village, led by the headman, had come to criticise her for walking around on her own with a man who was obviously no relative of hers.

Non retreated to her room and gazed at the moon rising over the distant mountains. Could she really stay here? Even worse thoughts, about whether her love for Takeo was an illusion or a poem she had read somewhere forgetting the author, she brushed aside. He seemed distant, beyond the moon.

At some time during the night she must have lain down

on her mattress and fallen asleep in her clothes. She was
woken by chill light and a touch of frost in the air. Startled,
she got up to wash and change into fresh clothes for work.

She was called to breakfast and handed her soup in
silence. She fixed her attention on the sound of the boy
slurping. Grandmother muttered something and walked
into the kitchen.

Mr Kumamoto translated: 'She says it is not necessary to
make so much criticism.'

Non relaxed slightly and felt warmth returning to her
face and hands. Mr Kumamoto switched the TV on,
irritably.

Silence continued, punctuated by short bursts of speech
from the television as Mr Kumamoto switched from channel
to channel. He finally turned it off.

'Oh yes,' he said. 'We have to go to the town hall tomorrow. They not know what to do. So they take time and get
excited. They even write to Tokyo to ask what they should
do!' He laughed and turned up the oil-stove.

'What do you mean?' she asked, dreading some worse
development.

'They ready to give you alien registration card,' Mr
Kumamoto said. 'They need your sign and fingerprints.'

She released the breath she was holding so tightly. It was
only about a card. 'Fingerprints?' she queried.

'You have to forgive them so slow – already two mons,'
he said. 'But you first alien who ever lived here.'

French Leave

E. ANN RUTHERFORD

Victoria Station – a black, bleak January day. Two people
clutched in a parting embrace: he tall, hook-nosed and
vulpine, broad shoulders slightly stooped, she much shorter,
dark blonde ringlets falling on her shoulders. She wears a
dark green pigskin coat stretched tightly across ample
bosom and hips; he's in a black ankle-length overcoat which
gives him a sinister air. The rain bounces off the slick slippery
railway track, blackened by years of spilt diesel. The sickly
smells of hot metal, diesel, dampness and smoke fill the
winter air, and the crowds huddled against the cold look
pinched: damp clothes, damp eyes. The bright lights and
posters on the blackened walls do nothing to counter the
overall air of greyness and misery.

We await the departure of the Boat Train. Feeling brave
and adventurous, I had decided to make the journey to
Victoria on my own, refusing John's offer to see me off, and
had boarded the train at Rhyl alone. By the time I changed
trains at Crewe my resolve had weakened, and by the time
I arrived at Victoria I was ready to retreat; I had never been
to London before. Then, out of the crowd, came John's long
familiar form swooping down on me, his black overcoat
flapping like Dracula's.

'I had to come', he said, his eyes aglow and certain that I
had regretted declining his offer.

Picking up my suitcase, he leads and I follow towards

the Left Luggage lockers – after only five minutes he has taken charge and I follow gratefully and meekly like a lamb. Hurrying through the crowded station, luggage safely stored, we emerge onto the wet, windy London street and cross the road through the heavy traffic to the bright inviting lights of a Wimpy Bar.

Reaching for my hand across the sticky cluttered table he smiles and says 'Well, Annie, you're really going?'

'It looks that way', I reply, feeling sick and distant, 'I've got my ticket in my bag, but I just don't know if I can board the train.'

Reaching into the never-ending pockets of his funereal black coat he hands me a small brown bottle of Valium. 'Take a couple of these – they'll make you feel better. You need them more than I do.'

As I take the proffered bottle I know I have no real use for its contents, but it's so much a part of our life together that I put it gratefully into my handbag, thankful for a reminder of him. I remember the last time we'd met.

A dull December day, the two of us walking side by side along the wintry promenade of the Welsh holiday resort – my home town – empty now of all but vague echoes of summertime, the summer smells of candy-floss, hot dogs and doughnuts all replaced by salt sea and desolation. After passing boarded-up rock-stalls and amusement arcades we had come on a photo-machine, surprisingly still in operation. Rummaging in our pockets we found the necessary change, and after checking our wind-blown woebegone images had dived into the booth, vieing for position in front of the blank screen. Giggling, we pressed the button and waited as the machine sprang into flashing and gurgling life. Tumbling out of the booth after the fourth flash we stood shivering and waiting.

This was to be our last day together. I remember how we

still pretended to be in love and that we still enjoyed our time together, talking of desolation and despair at the prospect of separation – he protesting that he would miss me and die without me. We had shared our dreams and desires for so long: bare bodies, bare hearts and souls, we had no secrets from each other save the creeping realisation that love had only ever been mutual need and wanting. The machine began to belch forth the fruits of its labours and looking at the shiny strip in his hand I saw the two of us trapped in time, smiling, lying through our teeth, together for ever: his image staring at me flat and empty.

He, seeing the same image, hoped I would change my mind and melt and soften with the illusion of togetherness so that we could pretend our lives. He tore the glossy strip in two, and I faltered as he offered me my half, wanting no part of the illusion but knowing that in time I might need a keepsake. I had taken the photo and reluctantly hidden it in my wallet.

'Are you taking sugar these days?' John offers me the sugar, wondering if my perpetual diet is on or off at present, and assuming from my present large proportions that I have lapsed yet again.

'Yes. I need it today, diet or no diet.'

'You'll be OK. You won't want to come home once you get into the swing of it.' We drink our coffee in silence.

I am unable to sit still, wanting desperately to be gone from here and away from this man who has refused to allow me out of his life, despite my protestations. I am glad of his company now, but wish he would give me my freedom.

We drift out into the cold street to the station, retrieve my two shabby cases, and hurry to the platform where the train is already standing. For months he has begged and pleaded with me to reconsider my decision to leave and yet here he is, pushing me forward – punishing me?

I get on the train and slam the door behind me, stow my luggage and then station myself at the half-open window.

'You will write, darling?'

'Of course I will, angel, you know I will.'

Finally the whistle blows, the train shudders; we hug, his eyes fill with tears and, seeing his sorrow, my own respond. As the train begins to move, he takes his hands away from mine, blows a kiss, and then turns and quickly loses himself in the crowd. Opening my handbag I check again my passport, travellers' cheques and ticket; seeing the small brown bottle I take it out, pour the contents into my palm and pop one into my mouth. After all, it can only help, can't it? At Dover, through my drug-induced torpor, boarding the boat is painless and even a little amusing as I find myself a safe-looking place and install myself and my luggage in one of the no-smoking lounges.

'Is this seat taken, dear?' A nice old lady, grey hair, silver-rimmed spectacles: someone's granny visiting Abroad for the first time. I steel myself.

'Are you going on your holidays, dear? I live in Paris. I've been to stay with my daughter and her children for Christmas, but I'll be glad to get home. Where did you say you were going?'

'To the south of France. Grasse, actually, to work as an au pair for six months.' Saying the words aloud is a way of trying to convince myself that this is really what I'm doing.

Asking the kindly lady to mind my bags I lurch my way towards the deck. Standing at the cold wet railings I search the horizon for signs of life, but see none except the scavenging gulls at my feet. I think of my life with John; after five years, my heart, soul and ego bruised, I had realised that only by putting a distance between us could I hope to start my own life, away from his powerful influence. As I stand at the railing my tears go unnoticed in the rain. I turn and carefully cross the slippery deck to return to my luggage.

What is Calais but Dover in reverse? As I disembark my ears are assaulted by the foreign sounds of words I know only from textbooks, spoken unintelligibly. I follow the crowd, wondering who will save me from all these aliens. The train journey south is long and dull except for two English girls (one a secretary in Milan, the other an au pair in Monaco) who take me under their wing and ply me with duty-free Drambuie. As the dawn breaks over Avignon I wake, feeling like death. In the grubby speckled mirror of the toilette I am confronted by a pale, drawn spectre; even my teeth look wrinkled. I curse my naïveté at not having packed clean knickers and, feeling dirty and dishevelled, prepare to enter polite French society. *Quelle femme fatale!*

As the train lurches to a halt at Cannes my heart lurches in sympathy. The two English girls help with the luggage; as the train continues its journey, I stand alone on the platform, lost. According to the agency's instructions, Monsieur B. is tall, grey, thirty-five, and will be wearing glasses and a black blazer. Clutching my crumpled instructions between my teeth, I drag my cases towards the exit gate.

'Pardonnez-moi, mam'selle'. Turning, startled, I am struck powerfully by the striking resemblance he bears to the other man I left at the other station. After several moments' attempts at conversation it becomes obvious that his English is much worse than my French. *Quelle domage*, as they say: a real shame. We shake hands and smile a lot and, taking my cases, he leads me out into the bright Riviera sunshine.

There are rows upon rows of palm trees along the promenade. We turn inland towards Grasse, passing pink and white houses surrounded by lemon trees, high walls and wrought iron gates. M'sieu B. drives as well as he speaks English. As we head for the hills I fumble for my seat-belt, only to be told, 'Oh, we don't bozzer wiz 'em 'ere – do you 'ave zem in Angleterre ?' I say a silent prayer.

We turn off down a dusty track and bump over pot-holes, leaving huge clouds of dust. Finally we stop outside a large rusty wrought-iron gate bearing the words La Retirada. This is it: *je suis arrivée*. As M'sieu B. struggles with the gate, my ears are assaulted by a loud alien gabbling from beyond, followed by the appearance of my soon-to-be charges racing to be the first to reach Papa and the new *fille*. I am overawed by the speed with which they speak French. Suddenly they freeze as a sharp staccato voice yells something totally unintelligible and the two little girls retreat to join their Mama.

Mme. B. is tiny and 'French-looking', with beautiful auburn hair cut into a short neat bob, her full lips curving down at the corners. I watch as she takes in my crumpled trousers, tousled hair and smeared make-up; as I look at her neat slim figure I wish I had stuck more rigorously to my diet.

'You must be tired, poor sing, come and put down your bags zen you can have a shower and a rest. We are going out so you can have some time to recover. Follow me: I will show you your room. Henri-Paul, take Annie's bags and put them in her room.' Dutifully picking up my cases, M'sieu B. follows the lady of the house. My room turns out to be a cabin in the garden.

'We will leave you now to unpack. When you are ready, please come and use the basroom.' They are gone and, finally alone, I look round the room. It contains one or two expensive-looking antique pieces of furniture – a highly-polished walnut desk, a carved wooden chest. The tiled floor gives the room a slightly cell-like atmosphere but I tell myself that once it is filled with my possessions it will feel like home.

There is a light tap on the door; Mme.B stands there, bearing a tray with coffee, French bread and an assortment of strange smelly cheeses.

"'Ere is your lunch, we are going out now. You can have a shower if you like. Dinner is at eight o'clock.'

I thank her and retreat to the bed with the tray, looking glumly at the crusty crumbly bread, the lukewarm muddy coffee and the sour-smelling sweaty cheeses. I torture myself with visions of my family, probably at this moment sitting down to Sunday lunch of roast beef and Yorkshire pudding. When the alarm-clock rattles my brain the next morning I lie under the scant bedclothes watching my breath forming little clouds in the icy air, and have to force myself into the chill morning. I let myself into the house, where breakfast fills the air.

In the kitchen the children are already at table surrounded by cereal packets and crumbs. The cornflakes are stale, the coffee too strong and the children spoilt, and if breakfast isn't bad enough my next job is to wash and dress them while they complain bitterly in words I have little difficulty understanding. Once this enormous task is completed Madame emerges, brusquely informs me of my chores for the day and vanishes into the blue yonder leaving me alone to cope as best I can with her two little darlings.

Alone together, the children and I soon establish an easy rapport and it becomes increasingly obvious that Anna, with her big brown eyes and cheeky grin, is everyone's favourite while plain, serious-looking Emanuelle hides behind her little pink spectacles and is unnoticed. I see in her my own four-year-old self as I watch her constant struggles to gain her mother's affection which is so lavishly bestowed on her sister.

As the days merge into weeks our days fall into a pattern, with sunny mornings spent walking in the nearby country lanes or visiting the playground or parks, and afternoons in the garden. My evenings belong to me and I spend them writing long sunny letters home to my family and friends and of course John. Finding myself growing daily in confidence I begin to enjoy my time off and venture further and further afield, visiting Nice, Grasse and Cannes and practising my faltering French with more and more panache. My skin begins to turn a pale golden honey and the weight begins to fall away almost visibly.

I meet Tony when, late for my weekly French lesson, I dive onto his departing bus amid loud cheers and a round of applause. His deep brown eyes smile mischievously at me from under a heavy fall of black hair. He jokes with his passengers and his handsome boyish face breaks into a teasing grin as he gestures for me to sit down – apparently I am to be treated to a free ride. At the bus terminus he introduces himself as Antoine and invites me to join him for coffee but I decline in embarrassment and lose myself in the crowd. During the next couple of weeks he haunts me like some demon driver – whenever I catch a bus he seems to be grinning devilishly at me from behind the wheel. At last, worn down by his persistence and his beautiful liquid brown eyes, I agree to meet him for supper.

Naturally we arrange to meet at the bus station and when I arrive, nail-bitingly nervous, I am grateful to see he is already these, looking truly amazing in dark blue sweater and pale blue slacks, Kissing me on both cheeks he takes me by the hand:

'Viens avec moi – on va manger' (Come with me – we're going to eat). Unsure as to whether I like his caveman approach I follow and over pizzas our conversation, although limited, becomes freer as the wine loosens our tongues and my somewhat battered French dictionary is passed back and forth across the formica table. By the time coffee is

served, thick and black, I find myself responding to his warmth; the months of loneliness, so long unacknowledged, well up inside me, and I know already that if he asks me back to his room I will go – I need to go on gazing into those deep sad brown eyes, want to be loved and feel desired, feel the warmth of his breath on my face and neck. I need to hold him close.

His small rented room is shabby and seedy; the tall scruffy building, like the others around it, smells strongly of some strange pungent herb, garlic and garbage. The room is dominated by a large sway-backed bed with brass knobs and a sagging mattress. There is a makeshift kitchen, separated from the rest of the room by a once-bright cotton curtain; there is a cracked sink and a greasy misused cooker. I know that my decision has already been reached; my agreeing to come here has said it all, and he expects payment in full for the dinner. We parry for a while; pure aching desire shines out at me from his eyes and it is this desire, and this alone, that I crave. I let his passion and his lust override my self-made rules, allowing him inside my empty aching body, and all the while thoughts of home cause the tears which flow deeply down my cheeks. He, delighted to have created such uncontrollable ecstasy and emotion, falls asleep.

During the following weeks he shares most of my free time. I plan my bus journeys to coincide with his work timetable, and during his breaks we spend endless hours passing my French dictionary across innumerable sticky coffee-stained café tables, while he fills my everpresent notebooks with letters and poems for later translation. I become increasingly fond of this warm, loving boy who appears so hurt and lost after the recent break-up of his marriage; I find comfort in offering him comfort, feeling towards him as I would to a stray puppy lost in the street.

He, however, begins to talk of marriage and our future, saying that he has told his family all about *la blonde* and that they are anxious to meet me, despite the fact that I am not a Catholic. We argue, he cries, shouts, rages, slams out of the room and, strangely, never seems to drive any bus I catch from that time on.

Daily I receive long laborious letters from John declaring his undying love. My bruised ego feels soothed, until I receive a letter from my mother which informs me that the two of them have been discussing wedding plans; she is worried lest I choose anywhere but the local parish church for fear of upsetting my father. Alone at the opposite end of the continent I feel helpless and manipulated; I begin to dread the letters from home and choose to be out at the arranged time of John's suffocating long-distance phone calls.

As the sun gradually gains strength with the onset of spring we embark upon day-long excursions to the *plage publique*, although Mme. B. insists that the French never indulge in such follies as going to the beach out of season. I grow to love Cannes, its social strata as clearly defined and separated as rock layers beneath the earth's crust. Topsoil consists of the rich summer people, seasonal visitors who moor their cruisers and air their candy-pink villas: rich, dark, fertile. The next layer is made up of emigrés: middle-class Parisians, adaptable as clay, willing to endure any hardship for the sake of being seen to live in the south of France (and my own *famille* are among them). Finally, at the bottom, the rock layer consists of the actual inhabitants of the Midi, warm in temperament like Tony, speaking with a thick syrupy almost unintelligible accent. These are the people who make life possible in their towns – bus drivers, refuse collectors, road sweepers, postmen, small farmers eking out a living on the all-but-barren soil, their shanty farms dotted incongruously among the bouganvillea-clad villas, clinging to the thought of what was once theirs. Grasse provides the perfect counter-balance to Cannes's high-powered chic, and I find myself drawn to this peaceful medieval town, spending hours wandering down its narrow cobbled streets. The town is filled with the sweet heady scents of mimosa, lily of the valley and jonquil.

I find my thoughts turning to home. I wonder what's happening in Coronation Street, and long to hear a Welsh accent. I wish I could wake up to hear the sound of rain battering my windows and feel the chill damp of a Welsh winter, but John's persistent entreaties for me to return home early only make me more determined to stay the course. Just as I am beginning to enjoy my life-style in this privileged French household, fate takes a hand in the form of *la grippe* (flu), which indeed grips me in a feverish stranglehold, leaving me weak and bronchitic and totally non-productive. I spend a fortnight in bed unable to eat or drink, and it becomes increasingly obvious that Madame is not prepared to pay for the pleasure of nursing an invalid and that I must return home. I shall miss the sunshine.

On the boat I spend the entire crossing on deck waiting for my first glimpse of Dover. I wonder if John will recognise me; I have lost over two stone through lack of proper food plus *la grippe*. At Victoria Station I struggle with my bags towards the exit gate.

'Annie, Annie!' John's not-so-familiar form is rushing towards me. He looks shorter and his nose is larger and his hair thinner than I remember, and instead of the sudden surge of joy I had expected to feel as he kisses me, I stay cold. I know now that my future is not with this man, and I feel strong enough to face it alone. As we walk towards the exit I don't know how I will tell him this, but now at last I know that I can.

Not Quite Yellow and Not Quite Blue

SUSAN RICHARDSON

July 1st 1994
International Women Playwrights' Conference – Day One. Much discussion of roots/identity, plus a story-telling workshop at the Aboriginal Cultural Centre. Theme of the workshop was 'Home' – most of the women told stories about the places/people they'll be returning to on Friday at the end of the conference.

My story was about not being able to go back to Wales for a year and having to think of Adelaide as home even though I've only just arrived. Tried to express how excited I feel to be attached to the University as Visiting Playwright, as well as how nervous.

July 29th 1994
Researched at the University till lunchtime, then moved into the room I've decided to rent on Myrtle Road – a large, sunny house with a garden full of lemon trees and wind chimes, plus a dog called Harmony who won't stop barking.

Melanie and her boyfriend, Dave, welcomed me with a rather fearsome-looking meal of black beans, bean curd, and some other bean-based item. My foreboding increased when I opened one of the kitchen cupboards just now and spotted six packets of Chinese medicine 'for very painful diarrhoea'.

Hope I've made the right choice by coming to live in this suburb by the sea instead of the city centre. I felt protected there somehow – all the grid-structured streets and well-pruned parks, I guess. Here, on the edge of the disorderly ocean, I feel very exposed.

August 1st 1994

Over a pot of Celestial Radiance tea, Mel informs Dave that it's time he did some Major Work On Himself. 'This morning, I want you to work on your sense of humour,' she says very seriously. 'Then later you can devote some time to your Emerging Artist.'

I manage to avoid seeing What Emerges by going for a long walk on the beach. Lots of empty shells, the flesh of their insides pecked out by birds. Big brittle razor-shells, crushed underfoot to nothing.

Research today a bit slow – found it really hard to focus.

October 8th 1994

Though I know I should be ploughing on with research and starting to conceive an overall framework for my play, I skived off and went to the Women, Power and Politics conference instead. It's been organised to commemorate 100 years of Women's Suffrage in South Australia – shocking to realise that women in the U.K. didn't get the vote until 24 years later. There's a real celebratory feel to the conference – a stirring session on 'Why Women Write' this morning, then an outdoor 'event', the end of Womentrek, this afternoon; a group of women have succeeded in walking the Heysen Trail – it's 1,000 km. long, I think – from the north of South Australia to the finishing point in the Adelaide Hills.

I managed all of 2 km. this evening, along the beach from the train station to Myrtle Road: dog-walkers, yachts, and the sea swallowing the sun like a giant orange Strepsil.

November 29th 1994

Started draft of the play: minimal progress. Brain over-heated and soggy – not sure how I'll survive the next three months of summer.

Ambled along the nature trail in the late afternoon – lots of sunburned tufts of stunted grass – and stopped at the kiosk for an ice-cream. Kids with bare feet and wet hair asking their mothers if they can have a Killer Python.

December 25th 1994

Beach walk, then Christmas lunch. Mel made something with chickpeas and millet. When he'd finished eating, Dave pronounced himself 'full as a Pommy's complaint box'. Harmony, still barking, got her usual bowl of veggies and rice.

Watched a video later – *The Russia House*. Didn't take in much of the plot, was too busy gawping at the landscape and the sky – patches of pale blue and a weak winter sun with bare trees silhouetted against it. The film was shot in Finland, I think, but the sky took me straight back to Wales.

January 28th 1995

My oldest – and probably most eccentric – ambition has finally been realised: I've seen an overseas Test Match. England are playing Australia at the Adelaide Oval, and there's much more razzmatazz here than at any game of cricket I've been to back home – parachutists landing on the outfield at lunchtime, a brass band playing at the tea interval. Lots of goodnatured bantering between the Australian and British fans, who seem to have come here in their thousands.

Reconnected with some of the journos I knew in my late teens when cricket journalism was the career-path I was determined to follow. Have been asked to write a human interest/crowd piece for one of the Sunday papers – will hopefully be able to squeeze it in between tomorrow's teaching sessions and working on my play.

January 31st 1995
England pulled off a stunning victory in the Test. The article I've put together is rather less spectacular, but I really enjoyed writing it and mingling with all the characters in the crowd.

'Australia's a great country,' said Colin-from-Essex, in a t-shirt advising everyone to *Save Water – Drink Beer*, 'but it'd be even better if it was the size of Britain. Or better still, the size of London. Then you could just get a cab to the Great Barrier Reef and hop on the Tube to Ayers Rock.'

March 13th 1995
Draft one of the play completed – not sure if I've incorporated enough of my research or tried to include too much.

Heat again brutal. 'Driest state in the driest continent, this is,' says Dave. 'Dry as a Pommy's towel.'

April 16th 1995
Did more work on second draft of play. Workshop at the South Australian Writers' Centre went smoothly – about ten people came and all want a follow-up session in a few months' time.

Mel's on a juice fast, hoping to 'purge her whole system and cleanse her whole digestive tract'. Dave's having none of it, and neither am I – I told her that I've got a Major Life Decision to make shortly and need rather more than juice to help me make it.

Though my twelve months as Visiting Playwright are coming to an end and the date when I planned to go back to Wales is approaching, I've been offered quite a lot of

work here in Adelaide for the coming year: more workshops at the Writers' Centre, some teaching at the University,
a writing residency with a women's Health Education Net-
work . . .

What to do – should I stay or should I go?

May 18th 1995
Gusty, blustery day: metallic grey sky and a stormy sea,
with angry, self-destructive waves hurling themselves at
the shore. Limp black seaweed and some stranded jellyfish
– big gelatinous blobs on the sand.

Wet-suited surfers skidding and scudding along. They
come into the kiosk dripping water, gobble pasties and pies
and hot dogs like they haven't eaten in days.

Think I'll stay.

July 1st 1995
International Drama-in-Education Conference, Brisbane.
Really stimulating mix of delegates, from Palestine, Croatia,
Vanuatu, Vietnam . . . Extraordinary atmosphere, too:
Kenyans initiated a spontaneous drumming and dancing
session in the foyer – about two hundred delegates kicked
off their shoes and joined in.

My workshop (Representing Women's Lives on Stage)
went well, but I felt it seemed really trivial in comparison
with some of the others. The most powerful presentation
was by a theatre group from the Philippines, about all the
young girls who've died there as victims of the sex
industry. Can't stop thinking about it.

July 16th 1995
'Hi, how ya doing?' says the American guy sitting next to
me on my flight back to Adelaide. He's wearing a t-shirt
proclaiming *I Dived the Reef.*

'Fine, thanks,' I reply.

'You from England?'

'No. Wales.'

'Oh.' He pauses. 'S'pose you speak Garlic then, do you?'

I bury my nose in the in-flight magazine to avoid any more of his attempts at conversation. Apparently the Editor's hoping to publish short crime fiction, and will pay $1,000 per story.

Reckon I'll give it a go.

August 29th 1995

Finished second draft of play; am at the stage where it needs to be workshopped – I need to hear it read aloud to get a sense of which bits of dialogue are working and which aren't.

Submitted crime story. Set it in a busy Australian airport – obnoxious passenger who thinks people in Wales speak Garlic gets murdered. Much enjoyed writing it but considering it's my first attempt at crime I don't have much hope of publication.

Mel's dragged Dave off to some sort of Sanctuary for a month-long silent retreat. She's left me in charge of Harmony, who's also blissfully silent. The big plateful of meat I gave her for dinner may well have something to do with it.

October 2nd 1995

In Tasmania for a week as writer-in-residence. Lanky, ginger-bearded taxi-driver who picked me up at Hobart Airport got very excited when I told him I'm from Wales. 'No way!' he said. 'I used to work the night-shift at Tesco's in Chepstow!'

October 10th 1995

Spent my last day in Tasmania, after all the workshops

were over, in Swansea! It's a settlement on the east coast, much smaller and sleepier than its Welsh namesake. Nearby Freycinet National Park is every bit as dramatic as the Gower peninsula though, especially Wineglass Bay with its arc of white sand and pink granite rock formations.

Got back to Adelaide to find a woman I've never seen before at the kitchen table, reading a book called *Vibrational Healing: Volume One*.

'Hi, I'm Jade, a friend of Mel's.' She closed her book, and looked me up and down a bit. 'Don't I know you from somewhere?'

'I don't think so.'

'You look very familiar. Where are you from?'

'Wales.'

'Wow! I've always wanted to go to Wales.'

I loaded some of the clothes from my case into the washing-machine. 'Are you from Adelaide?'

'Yeah, it's a fantastic city – I don't ever want to leave. Unless I can go to Wales, of course. I'd kill to go to Wales.'

I put some washing-powder in the machine.

'You've got great vibes,' she went on. 'I feel very comfortable around you. Are you sure we haven't met before?'

'I'd remember you if we had,' I said, and switched the machine on.

She continued staring at me with her head on one side. 'We *have* met before, you know,' she said at last.

'Where?'

'Wales.'

'I thought you said you'd never been there.'

'I was there in a past life.'

Beat a hasty retreat to my room, did the rest of my unpacking and sorted through my mail. Great news – my crime story's been accepted for publication by the in-flight magazine!

November 15th 1995
Evening walk – dried apricot sky, flat sunbaked sand, sea with lazy waves that barely seem to be trying.

An Adelaide theatre group have offered to do a rehearsed reading of my play in early January. Feel so lucky to have this opportunity – for some reason, I don't have to fight so hard to make things happen here as I do back in Wales.

December 26th 1995
Strange to be camping and not to need sleeping bags and extra clothes – strange to wake up with emus strutting around the tent, too. And strange to see the pink water of the Pink Lake on the way here from Adelaide; it's surrounded by salt deposits which look just like snow and sound just like snow – walking on them, I mean – snow of the crunchy, crisp, long-frozen kind. Glad it isn't snow, though, from the point of view of the temperature.

January 10th 1996
Sensational start to the New Year: my crime story's been shortlisted for a Scarlet Stiletto award! May have a go at a longer piece of crime fiction – once I re-work my play, that is. The rehearsed reading was really helpful – I've got a much clearer idea now of which scenes need fixing.

March 6th 1996
Adelaide Festival – the biggest celebration of the Arts in Australia. Like the rest of the city I've become nocturnal, trying to see as many plays, concerts and fringe events as possible. At midnight we all spill out of the theatres and head for the outside performance space – wonderfully, it's still warm enough for just t-shirt and shorts. At 1 a.m. large-scale street theatre gets underway – last night it was a building-site ballet with a crane and an earth-mover performing a *pas de deux*!

During the day I'm at Writers' Week, wandering from marquee to marquee, seeing Malcolm Bradbury, Sue Grafton, J. M. Coetzee, E. Annie Proulx . . . Unlike the Hay-on-Wye festival and every other literary event I've ever been to, all sessions are completely free. Many of the readings and discussions I've listened to seem to be on the subject of emigration/place – much to think about.

April 12th 1996
Taught what may be my last workshop here. One of the participants thought from my voice that I'm Australian.

May 14th 1996
Department of Immigration said no to an extension of my visa.
    Only 25 days to go.

May 25th 1996
Last time I'll see Dave – he has to go to Melbourne for a month of business. 'Busy as a one-legged arse-kicker, me.' Before he leaves he gives me a present: a boomerang bearing the label 'Flight tested – it WILL come back.'

June 5th 1996
Mel's having one of her psychic days. 'I've had a vision of you coming back to Adelaide in two years' time,' she says.
    'Really? Just for a holiday, or for longer?'
    'Oh, I can't divulge all the details. The messenger should never do that.'

June 7th 1996
Final beach walk. Final sunset. Overhead the sky's blue-black, paling towards the horizon. A strip of orange fading to yellow reaches up to touch the blue. The intersection

between yellow and blue – that's the point that fascinates me. It produces a colour which has no name – not green, as you might expect, but a blue-yellow. A colour that's not quite yellow and not quite blue. A colour that has something of both, but is neither. A colour which, while drawing from its two contrasting origins, is uniquely and entirely itself.

V

HERE BECAUSE OF MY HUSBAND

The pieces in this chapter were written by Welshwomen whose experiences abroad came about because they married men who worked in, or came from, countries outside Britain; unlike, for example, the women who decided to work or spend time travelling in a particular country, these contributors chose the man rather than the place. Their accounts demonstrate that in some ways this situation can be easier than that of a woman travelling or living abroad on her own – a wife will not usually need to justify her presence in the foreign community, since it will be taken for granted that she is there because her husband is there – but may also in some ways be more difficult: she may well have less freedom as to where she goes and how long she stays there, to say nothing of the fact that her behaviour may be taken to reflect on her husband and if it is thought to be inappropriate he may suffer.

Within this group of married women, however, there are major distinctions to be made and several are represented here: between going with your husband to his country of origin and going to a country foreign to you both; between going to your husband's country of origin when you expect it to be your permanent home, and going there on an extended visit; between accompanying your husband when he is sent to a place where there is a well-established expatriate community, and going with him when the impulse to move to another country comes entirely from him and when the two of you will be the only people from outside the community you are living in; between going to live in a place where the community around you speaks a language you know well, and to a place where you have to come to terms wih a new language as well as a new culture.

The response of the foreign community to the incoming wife can also vary widely. The most important thing for members of the community which the Welshwoman in Michigan enters is that she fits into their patterns of work and social behaviour, while the Welshwoman in Kenya is part of the school community through her work as a teacher but also has her close family unit (which, moreover, speaks a different language from the other expatriates around them) as a focus for her life there. The Welshwoman visiting Serbia is regarded by some of the people she meets there as a representative of Britain (in relation to visas and money) rather than as a person in her own right, but this also enables her to get away with behaviour that a Serbian could not. The Welshwoman in Crete is expected to demonstrate at least some of the skills and behaviour of a good Cretan wife, both by the women of the village (in relation to her domestic skills) and by the men, who accept her presence in the male preserve of the village café because she is there to interpret for her non-Greekspeaking husband, and so is fulfilling her traditional wifely role of serving him.

There is considerable variety in their experiences and in their response to them, but they all share a need both to respond appropriately to the new communities they find themselves in and at the same time to retain their own identities, of which their national identity is an important part.

The Calico Year

MAUREEN BELL

Thousands of feet below me Eire's green fingers released the silver Atlantic, and seven hours later I was met by my fiancé Ron in Michigan. I had gone through a barrier not only in time but also in space.

Ron had been released early from the armed services and had gone back home. I had completed my teaching year before joining him. We were to stay with Ron's parents until our wedding.

Burnt-white, mile-square fields pulled the eye to the horizon whichever way I looked. Dust-trails feathered the skyline (probably farmers in pickups or kids joyriding in Ford Mustangs, I was told). No trees. I could hear the slow homing thunder of combines, prairie liners, moving majestically into port. Skin-stripping bales of hay were being stacked barn-high. At the near end of the barn, a huddle of rough-tongued calves pressed shoulders when they heard the clanking pails of whey.

Inside the shimmering white farmhouse Grace, my future mother-in-law, was moving painfully through the steam. She had just finished canning eighty quarts of tomatoes against adversity. She and her husband, Ed, had cleared the land of trees and scrub and built the house with the timber themselves. Solid as stones, they endured blizzards, hurricanes and blistering heat impassively,

Ed and Grace had perfected a marital ballet, choreographed through forty years of living together. She would scream at him and he would retaliate by driving the tractor near her washing and showering it with red earth. Ed had a momumental appetite. I only ever heard him raise his voice once; after eating three sizeable steaks between six doorsteps of bread, he asked for more. On being told that there was nothing else he stormed out shouting, 'A guy cain't get a thing to eat round here!' He was a man of few words: each spring he would say, to the rocking of his chair, 'Spring's a-comin. Yep, she's a-comin.' And in autumn, 'Winter's a-comin'. Yep, she's a-comin'.'

It was said that Grace was a woman not many people could get along with. However, because Ron went to work early and didn't get home till late, I spent my first weeks in Michigan in her company; that we seemed to rub along together was a tribute to her forbearance. Possibly my eagerness to learn as much about her way of life as I could flattered her. Her only comment about me, made to her daughter Bea (and relayed back to me) was, 'She's alright, but her skirts is too short.'

'That's just her belly, Maw!' replied Bea.

I was five months pregnant; when making my maternity clothes I hadn't allowed for the belly. I was so proud of my full-bodied state that I not only sewed lace around the hems but also embroidered a flower over the 'bump'. When Ron and I had moved in together I screwed up enough courage to ask a doctor for contraceptive advice. 'If you sleep with every Tom, Dick and Harry you must expect to get pregnant,' was the only 'advice' she gave me. Next, I tried the Family Planning Clinic, but it was so discreetly located that I couldn't find it. I mentioned contraception to Ron but was so embarrassed that it was very much easier to sleep together without it. He told me later that he'd hoped I'd get pregnant so I'd have to marry him.

The prospect of giving birth frightened me, but my hunger to have a baby was so powerful that it overrode the fear. When the test results were positive I did four cart-wheels in the park. When I telephoned my parents to tell them the news, all my normally puritanically-strict father said was, 'Make sure you get plenty of fresh fruit and vege-tables.'

I had arrived in the hottest part of the year. When I rose at seven in the morning the smooth blond floorboards were already warm to my feet and the sun was releasing the aromatic pine resin that tickled my nose. By ten the clothes stuck to my back. Housework was done first thing in the morning; after that, time was spent showering and drink-ing Verners Ginger Ale in ice-frosted glasses on the back porch. Often we would go visiting or grocery-shopping. Air rushing through the car windows gave an illusion of coolness, so I looked forward to these trips.

The landscape made me very uneasy. In Wales my view had always been bounded by green hills or trees; here there was no end to the view in any direction. I was drowned in space. It also took me a long time to get used to addressing people by their first names. Even children did it; they had a status equal to adults. It stemmed from Frontier days, when every human being was valuable in the ceaseless struggle against the encroaching wilderness. Partly for that reason women, also, had more status and power than in Wales.

The equivalent to the corner shop at home, Maples General Store, was five miles away. During the five years I lived in Michigan I never found anything that Esther Maple didn't stock. Grace went there for anything not available in the local grocery store, and petrol.

Once a fortnight Grace would shop for food in a town fifteen miles away. Winnegan boasted a bank, a hardware store, a drugstore with a soda fountain, a food supermarket and four streets of houses. We would load up the car with the brown paper grocery bags, have an ice-cream at the soda fountain, and set off for home. I could have enjoyed myself walking round the town, but Grace wouldn't stay: 'I don't like the city,' she said brusquely. However, on the way back we would stop at the fruit-stall (in fact, a wooden building at the side of the road) to buy fruit and vegetables or just to drink a long cool glass of frothy black root-beer. Even before I entered it, I caught the fragrance of peaches picked in the sharp dawn. Once inside, there were baskets of canteloupes and honey-dew melons, golden corncobs, crimson peppers . . . I would have no difficulty following my father's advice.

One morning I saw the little silver flag on our mail-box raised: in it was a card from Bucks Blueberry Acres saying that the crop was ready. So with three carloads of relatives and as many pails as could be found, we went blueberry-picking. We harvested until the bushes danced before our eyes in the heat, paid, and took our booty home. All but a few were for the freezer. Next morning, however, I was drawn to the kitchen table by the scent of chilled blue-berries in a white china bowl, tumbled in milk and sugar.

Although there was a cornucopia of food for my body, my mind had nothing to chew on. Grace got a local but not a national paper. The local TV and radio stations turned out a bland diet of game-shows and soap operas. There were no books in the house, and no library nearer than twenty-five miles away. Eventually I found a box of *Readers' Digest* condensed novels under the stairs, and devoured them.

During the harvest all the neighbouring farmers came to help, and the women came too. In the evening they cooked huge meals, but during the day they would set up Grace's quilting-frame and have a quilting bee. As they quilted they would piece together stories and gossip as colourful as the calico they sewed.

Ron had his own difficulties. After being his own man for four years while he was away, he was now back with his parents and being treated like a child. It was as if he had to go through the process of being a rebellious teenager again, while at the same time I was expecting him to behave like The Head Of The Family. The friction between Ron and his mother upset me; almost as soon as he arrived home from work each evening he and Grace would be snarling and shouting at each other. I felt like ducking under the table. He was a linesman for a telephone company and his work took him all over the state; sometimes I went with him. Before our wedding he had to go to north Michigan; it was a place of wild forests and red-gold earth, of wolverines, bears and rattlesnakes. I was used to the austere majesty of Snowdonia and these hills were lower than I had expected, but the air was much cooler and sweeter than at the family's homestead.

Grace organised a shower for me, a female rite that men kept well away from. All the many relatives came from the length and breadth of the state; they loved a get-together. I had curiosity value: Grace had always claimed that her Ron was too good for any woman, and now I had ensnared him. Tables were stacked with the presents they brought: sheets, towels, household equipment of all kinds. I was very grateful; we couldn't have afforded to buy them ourselves. The women were formidable in their size, in their upswept diamanté glasses, their powder and perfume and lilac-tinted hair, but their good humour and laughter filled the house.

Ron had bought us a trailer in a trailer-park landscaped with lawns and trees, just outside a small town thirty miles away from the farm. I thought it was beautiful. I remember September 20th, our wedding day, as a day suffused with gold. I felt as fruitful as Autumn. It was my distinct impression that I held Ron up during the ceremony. His hand was icy.

Apart from us and the priest and altar-boy there were just our two friends, Mike and Betty, who acted as witnesses. Grace and Ed didn't come and wouldn't speak to us for weeks after the wedding; because they wouldn't talk to us, we didn't know why. Mike thought he had seen them outside the church. I think that when they realised we were to be married in a Catholic church they were too afraid to go in.

Ron's sister Bea got him a job at the bowling alley where she worked as a short-order cook. It meant we were solvent again, but we didn't see much of each other: Ron was working thirteen hours a day and I did some baby-sitting until I became too tired. As big as a barn, I sailed in and out of the doctor's office.

Sharp frosts released sugar-beet from the claggy earth. Throughout the November murk we saw leviathan lorries with triple tyres garner the late harvest by floodlight. Then the snows came.

One morning at three o'clock I sensed a slight tightening and releasing of tension in my back. It was like the distant drumming of an approaching army. I woke Ron, who telephoned the doctor, and we sped off to the hospital through a white world. They put me on a high bed in a bare room. Soon I had no consciousness of myself as a person, but only as a repeatedly-dynamited shatter of red pain. Masked, hooded faces moved in and out of my view. No one spoke to me.

Straining with what appeared to be coal-tongs, they pulled out a slippery purple object and put it on my stomach.

I was fascinated to see it turn red and hear it croak like a frog. I thought I would never be afraid of anything again, not even death. The baby and I were complete as an egg. That evening stays fresh in my mind because it was the most peaceful time of my life. Ron came to visit, unshaven and smelling of beer. He brought not flowers but bills for me to work out.

I brought baby Patrick home through the snow. My mother had sent me a large parcel of baby clothes, and I spent as much time reading the local newspaper that padded the box they came in as admiring the clothes. It was the nearest I ever got to homesickness.

With the rest of the family we went to the farm for Christmas. Trestle tables were set up in the basement and we ate our way through beef, pork and fowl. I stole away upstairs from the family games to read in Ed's big arm-chair, Patrick sleeping next to me in a carry-cot. I caught balloons of happy chatter as they floated up through the heating vents.

Snow muffled sound, wiped out all colour and trapped me in my rapidly-shrinking trailer. Some days the sun never rose. Looking out from the trailer early one morning I saw deer tracks near the door, while in the distance white tails disappeared below the slender black birches; they were so hungry they braved human contact. A plump skunk, humbug-striped, made its stately undisturbed progress to the incinerator each day. Just as I thought the snow was permanent it became sluggish and wet. The land, pale and wasted, struggled, like Lazarus, free of its winding-sheet.

We had enough money now to go out together sometimes, so I found us a baby-sitter: Irene Laplante, a tiny twinkling Chippewa Indian. Her trailer was piled high with scraps of calico that she made into rugs. There was an iron stove burning, with a cast-iron kettle and a skillet on it.

In two weeks the temperature went from below zero to the seventies and eighties Farenheit. The snow was a pale ghost from the distant past and nothing to do with us. We were all looking forward to a summer of fruitfulness and pleasure: another calico year was waiting to be patchworked together.

Serbian Summer

PAULA BRACKSTON

In 1996 I married a Serb in Britain, and the following summer we decided to try out his new visa and visit his family in Belgrade. Knowing that few Yugoslavs speak English I had spent months trying to master the basics of his language, and was looking forward to experiencing a new land and a new culture.

Serbia, together with its smaller neighbour Montenegro, is what is left of Yugoslavia. In the early 1990s its people were still numb with shock at having lost the Bosnian conflict, at being made international pariahs, and at having had their economy collapse. At the same time the country was eager to make the best of things and move on; I was lucky to visit in 1996 before the Kosovo crisis. Young people, in particular, were still enjoying a long love affair with 'western' culture with London at its centre, and pirated tapes of British pop music were everywhere.

My new husband's friends and relatives fell into two distinct groups as far as their interest in me was concerned. There were those who were curious about this pale, skinny British girl and slightly worried that I might dilute the Serbness of my husband Pedja, and then there was a much larger group who didn't care if I had two heads as long as I gave him a British visa; for these people I was a minor hero already and could do no wrong – which was just as well as I blundered about among them, murdering their beautiful, complex language and treading clumsily on their fragile post-war sensibilities.

My new mother-in-law and her husband had sweetly vacated their little flat (going to stay with her mother) so that we would have some privacy and independence during our visit. She had left food, including an enormous bowl of strawberries, in the fridge for us and I attempted to thank her in my juvenile Serbian; unfortunately the word for strawberries (*jagode*) is dangerously close to the most commonly-used swearword (*jebiga*), but she was kind enough to forgive my linguistic blunder and continued to encourage my efforts to speak the language.

A few days later the part of my brain which deals with language was tested nearly to breaking-point. I had arranged to meet Pedja at his grandmother's house and, as was invariably the case, he was late. Hours late (another quaint Serbian custom, it seemed).

As grandmother spoke no English, we had to battle on in Serbian – me stuttering, her shouting. Occasionally frustration would drive her to speak German, but unless the conversation was to be about Christmas trees or a little night-music, this was wasted on me. At three o'clock she explained, largely through mime and waving a TV schedule at me, that her favourite soap opera was about to start; relieved, I sat down to watch, thinking that at least I wouldn't have to struggle with the language for half an hour.

Which just goes to show how wrong you can be. The soap, it turned out, was imported from Venezuela, so that my ears were assaulted by Spanish, a language in which I could only order beer. The Serbian subtitles flashed up onscreen in the Cyrillic alphabet, which raised the unintelligiblity level for me even higher. I would happily have let it all wash over me and have continued to exist without ever knowing the triumphs and tragedies in the story of

'Cassandra', but Grandmother was having none of it. She was desperate that I should enjoy the programme so that, along with the Spanish soundtrack and the Serbian subtitles, I had to contend with a simultaneous translation into German. At high volume. I can state categorically that there were no Christmas trees (or nocturnal music, for that matter) involved.

The food was one of the aspects of life in Serbia which made me feel homesick. It is the Serb habit to eat meat three times a day rather than the three times a week I was accustomed to; they also use liberal amounts of pepper and chillis, so that I soon learned that *pola ljut* (half hot) lay somewhere between Madras and Vindaloo. I'm sure that *ljut* would have killed me. Everywhere I begged for *bez ljut* (without hot) – my own invention, a phrase which didn't really exist but at least occasionally resulted in something I could eat without suffering. By week ten I was writing desperate postcards home bearing only the words 'Send broccoli!' The two things I came to love were *ajvar*, a sweet pepper chutney (which is *bez ljut*), and *pljeskavica*. These were huge succulent burgers made with lamb or beef, always with a little added pork (to stop Muslims enjoying them, I was told), usually topped with a light cream cheese and served in a warm bread roll. These could be bought from street booths everywhere and were cheap and delicious. It was a measure of the influence of American culture at the time that when a McDonalds opened in Belgrade people deserted their national dish to queue for hours and spend a week's wages on a vastly inferior imitation.

The three things I had worried about before visiting Serbia had been – in no particular order – the police, the Mafia and the guns. My experiences of the police were certainly mixed. Out exploring in Belgrade one day I became lost in the city and, spotting two policemen, I followed my

British instincts and asked them for directions. They looked
a little surprised, but were helpful and extremely patient
with my Serbian. Pedja's family, however, was shocked to
hear what I had done: 'You do your best *not* to speak to a
policeman here,' my husband told me. 'You don't even
make eye-contact if you can help it. And you asked them
for directions? I'm amazed they didn't at least take away
all your papers.'

I was sceptical of this judgement of the police, but my
second encounter with them seemed to bear out his
opinion. We were driving with another couple to the coast,
to spend some time in Montenegro. On a lonely stretch of
road we were flagged down by a solitary uniformed figure.
Pedja told me that on no account was I to open my mouth;
if the policeman knew there was British money in the car
the 'fine' would treble. Our friend, who had been driving,
stood at the side of the road and listened as the policeman
informed him he had crossed a white line and would be
given a ticket; he would receive an order to pay a fine of
approximately £50 in a week or so. Zelko argued that this
represented a fortnight's wages to him, and that we were
just going away for a few days and didn't have much
money. After a great deal of sighing and tutting, the policeman gave him the option of an on-the-spot fine of about £5.
We watched him put the money in his back pocket before
he waved us on our way.

Guns were plentiful; everyone seemed to have one.
Walking down a busy Belgrade Street one sunny afternoon
I took no notice of what I thought was yet another back-
firing Zastava until I realised that everyone else was lying
on the ground or huddled in doorways: they knew the
sound of gunfire when they heard it, even if I didn't. No
one appeared to have been hit, and after a moment people
got to their feet, dusted themselves down, and went about

their business; normal life, such as it was, resumed. The week before we arrived the Chief of Police had been shot dead in front of his family in a restaurant two doors up from our flat. People were either gladdened or saddened, depending on their view of him, but no one was surprised.

During our stay in the family's apartment in the pretty seaside town of Budva in Montenegro an important football match took place. While the others watched it on TV I sat on the balcony writing postcards. When the game ended people came running onto the streets shouting and cheering. As I wrote to my aunt of how peaceful the little resort was, I heard what sounded like firecrackers but guessed was gunfire. When machine-gun fire joined the cacophony I was left in no doubt. My husband was furious: 'You don't go out on the balcony when they're shooting!' he told me, dragging me back inside. Silly me.

The Mafia were very powerful in Serbia at that time, and very obvious in Montenegro too; the difference was that there they were big fish only in their comparatively little pond. They were generally younger than those in Serbia, too; some of them had been at school with my husband. We had been in Budva for a day or two when Pedja arranged a meeting with one such old friend, who now owned a beachside nightclub. For some reason I now forget I arrived first, alone. I took a table and waited, for both Pedja and the mysterious friend.

My Serbian was passable by this time, so when I saw a likely-looking young man sit down at the next table I asked him, *'Da li si Gospodin Zetz?'* (Are you Mr Zetz?) He shook his head solemnly and told me that Mr Zetz would be arriving soon.

This would have been unremarkable but for two things. One was the unmistakable gun-shaped bulge under his jacket (he turned out to be the nightclub boss's right-hand man, known to have literally got away with murder). The other was that *Gospodin Zetz* translates as Mr Rabbit. It is difficult to take anyone called Mr Rabbit seriously, but I was definitely the only one laughing; luckily they thought I was an eccentric British woman and I was able to get away with it. When Mr Zetz finally arrived it was clear he was a fan of the *Godfather* movies and had modelled himself on Al Pacino, from his hairdo right down to his walk. In his mind he was living in a film, his money coming from who knows where and what, besides his popular nightclub.

On the twelve-hour journey from Belgrade to Budva we had driven through a constantly-changing landscape; we would be in open river plains one minute and vertiginous mountain passes the next. I was made keenly aware of crucial differences between life in the Serbian countryside and that in Wales where I grew up. At home there was a culture of living in the countryside while still pursuing a variety of careers; at the same time, people in Wales grew up with an affinity for and an appreciation of their surroundings, regardless of whether their interests lay in farming or elsewhere. Not so in Yugoslavia: the Serbs in particular have a very different view of the country from ours. No Serb would willingly consider living outside the city: the country is something you pass through to get from one city to another, or to reach your seaside apartment or ski resort; otherwise, you leave it to the peasants so that they can get on with the business of producing food.

At one point on our journey, as we neared a small lowland farm, the strong smell of manure invaded the car.

'Yuck! Cow shit!' exclaimed my companions.

'No—' I corrected them, '—not cows. Pigs.'

They stared at me, amazed. 'You mean you can tell what animals are on the farm by the smell of their shit?' Zelko asked me.

'Of course.'

I kept them amused for hours, correctly identifying cows, sheep, hens and horses by smell alone. You never know what is going to impress people when you're abroad.

By the end of my summer in Yugoslavia I felt I had a much clearer understanding of how my husband's mind worked, not least because I had glimpsed the enormous cultural differences between us. I was fascinated by the alternative perspective, the close family bonds, the passion and the resilience of the people. I began to see how different life was for people whose country is situated in a geographical and political corridor: invasion threatens from all directions and at any time. I greatly enjoyed learning the language, though I could have continued to do so for another ten years and still have left room for improvement.

I did at least have one small moment of linguistic triumph. One night, heading home in a taxi on my own, I struck up a conversation with the driver. After ten minutes or so of chatting he turned to me and asked, 'What part of Macedonia do you come from?' Serbian and Macedonian are sufficiently close for people on both sides of the border to converse without any difficulty; I may not quite have been talking like a native, but it was good enough for him!

Santa is a Welshman

GWENLLÏAN JONES

Trouble in Uganda sent us back to Britain and then to Kenya where my husband was to work. I was not too happy about this because I had stayed in Nairobi more than once, on shopping expeditions and on the way to Mombasa and the beach, and had formed a very unfavourable impression of the place. I was glad when John wrote from Nairobi to say we were to live in Nakuru, a country town. Soon after, Dafydd (who was three at the time) and I flew to Nairobi, where John was – predictably – late to meet us at the airport and Dafydd asked,'Is this my Daddy?' in Welsh every time a man on his own walked by.

Nakuru is much bigger today than it was then, in 1973. At that time the architectural style of the main street was very 'colonial', and the mainly single-storey shops, most of which sold dress material and clothes, had corrugated-iron roofs. There were three grocery stores, two of them stocking goods that were clearly well past their sell-by dates; the rust on the tins, the weevils in the flour and the colour of the butter in the fridge were clear evidence. The third shop was better, although the shopkeepers understandably hoarded goods (which was technically illegal) as insurance against the frequent shortages, and produced them furtively from the back of the shop for regular customers. Because of a long drought, at the time we arrived there was no butter for sale – one could see that the land was parched and desperately needed rain. There was an excellent bread shop kept by a Seychellois family; the market was full of fruit and vegetables – pineapples, pawpaws, beans and potatoes; you could choose your chicken while it was still alive, watch it being strangled, and take it home while the body was warm: and all this in a small country town.

A couple of miles down a road that ran under jacaranda trees, past our pleasant but rather sparsely-furnished home and through the tall stalks of corn, was Lake Nakuru with its thousands of pink flamingoes and pelicans. They always made me think of the verses in the Bible where Christ is compared to the pelican which gives its blood to feed its young, and gory images of crucifixes, crowns of thorns and the poetry of Ann Griffiths often made me momentarily uncomfortable at this beautiful place. Whenever we asked Dafydd on a Saturday or Sunday where he'd like to go, the answer was always '*y llyn*' (the lake). The great attraction was a huge colony of hyrax, rather plump and rat-like but essentially attractive creatures whose nearest relative is the elephant. They always sat sunning themselves on the same cluster of rocks and never ran away when we stopped the car and sat in it watching them. I can never remember them actually *doing* anything and hyrax-gazing was very limited as a spectator sport, but Dafydd loved it and would be completely lost in his admiration for them while John and I sweated nobly in the hot car. We also saw water buffaloes, various sorts of deer-type animals, and beautiful birds.

We made trips to the National Parks as often as possible: Masai Mara, Tsavo, Amboseli and Samburu. The last of these was my own favourite; in Samburu the people dressed very differently from the Kikuyu round Nakuru, and rode camels through their arid homeland. It was always a pleasure to see the Masai, in red ochre and red clothing, in their own part of the country and I doubt if there are better-looking young men anywhere in the world than the tall, stately Masai warriors. I was always on the lookout for one wearing a Bryncir Woollen Mill bed-cover which had been taken off our bed with a hook and pole and slid through a small opening in the window; the thief could easily have sold it to a Masai, knowing their penchant for all things red. Nakuru was once in the territory of the nomadic Masai herdsmen, and they were the people who had given it its name, which translates as 'the place of the dust devils'; because of the dust and the soda from the lake the Colonial Service had at one time regarded it as a hardship posting. Certainly Dafydd suffered a lot from tonsilitis while we were there.

One night a young man was killed in a brawl in the nightclub below John's office; I remember going to call on him at his work the following day and seeing dried blood on the stairs. The victim was the brother of a Somali friend of mine who taught at the same school as me; the owner of the school was a Kikuyu but all the teachers apart from Miriam were European. Pupils included Kenyans, Scandinavians, Indians, Germans, Japanese, Dutch, English and Americans, plus one small Welsh boy who at the beginning spoke no other language; the children were taught in English, and it took Dafydd three weeks to learn some of the language and six weeks to become fluent (a second language poses no problems when you are three years old). There were free places for some local orphans, and it was our job as a family to pick up two small girls from the orphanage every morning. The woman who ran the orphanage did her best with very little, but it was a cold, bare place. On the other hand, having a family was not always a recipe for happiness: a five-year-old in my class once told me that his father used to beat him every weekend as a warning of what would happen to him if he was naughty like his brother (the logic in beating a child both when he was naughty *and* when he wasn't defeated me). I loved the school, and I think it was the happiest place I ever worked in.

Father Christmas came every year, and for our first Christmas there he was a Welshman; Dafydd was thrilled that Santa could speak Welsh, as he was beginning to think that the three of us were the only Welsh-speakers in the world. At John's football club children's party that year another Welshman was Santa, and of course Dafydd took Santa's Welshness completely for granted. The next year John himself was the school Santa, and I remember him arriving on a tractor, sweating under his heavy costume, his cushion belly and his bushy beard in the heat. Dafydd told us that night that Santa had kind brown eyes just like his Daddy's. In the school nativity play Dafydd was a shepherd, and as the curtain closed for the interval he was left on the wrong side of it. Seeing me in the front row of the audience, he had the presence of mind to shout in Welsh, 'What am I supposed to do now, Mam?'

Nakuru was a good place to live in and so was our house, in spite of a horrible dog called Boy, which used to shit in the house, run away for days, and then come back covered in sewage and infested with fleas which contaminated the house and everything in it for a few days. We had a cheerful milkman who delivered milk in tetrapaks on a bike, and the Guava Man who sold fruit at the door. There were two tortoises in the back garden, the football club and a swimming pool close at hand, the huge and most marvellous country to explore, and hundreds of miles of empty, sandy beaches all the way up the coast. We went round Mount Kenya, saw the snows on Kilimanjaro, watched wild cheetahs running, smelt hyenas, and saw lions, elephants, rhinos and hippo; colobus monkeys swung in trees by the roadside. We saw amazing places, got to know good people, and see wonderful animals; once we even saw a black leopard. It was very difficult to say goodbye: even leaving the horrible dog made me cry. I missed the children at school, and to this day think of some of them and wonder what has become of them: where is Maina, the naughty and happy one, who must now be over thirty? Darminder, the tall Sikh boy? Jimmy Kandi, who said not one word to me for a whole year? At least I know where Dafydd is now – back in Africa.

Home Sweet Home

HEATHER JONES

In the first heady weeks of my new life abroad I felt only contempt for the life I'd left behind. From the paradise in which I now found myself, my Welsh homeland seemed grey, wet, windswept and unbearably dull. I wondered why I'd been full of misgivings the day my husband interrupted my comfortable post-menopausal life with an announcement: 'I *have* to do it, ' he said with the desperation only an artist can muster. 'I have to move to Greece to paint pictures.' In answer to my startled stream of questions on practicalities – where would we live? what would we live on? how long would we be away? – he tossed back his head in artistic pique and flounced into his studio.

We duly arrived in a village on the island of Crete, heaving our suitcases onto buses that seemed to leave when the driver thought there were enough passengers aboard. A bulging portfolio of paintings and a sleeping-bag kept slipping from my grasp. I felt like a refugee. After a hot day of bargaining and bartering we eventually found rooms in a house near the sea. We had visited the island twice before and fallen in love with its rugged beauty and unique history. The inhabitants, warmhearted and generous, are renowned for their friendliness. It is an island where *machismo* may be infuriating at times, but the charm of Cretan men is nonetheless endearing. Their desire to show strength and 'manliness' stems partly from a national admiration of the *palikari* (men who fought to defend the island against Turkish invaders) and partly from the belief every Greek male is born with, that he is irresistible. Despite the influx of tourists along some coasts traditions remain strong, family ties and honour are paramount, the numerous saints are revered and their feast-days observed. In the remote villages of the dramatic *Lefka Ori* (White Mountains) the people follow a lifestyle that has not changed for hundreds of years. *Philoxenia* (hospitality to the stranger) is an important word to a Cretan and the mountain people still extend a genuine welcome to any traveller who cares to pass the time of day with them, especially those who make an effort to master the complexities of their language.

Despite having studied Greek I soon discovered the difference between chanting to myself at home and trying to keep up with rapid conversation. I was never sure I had the gist of what was being said and lived constantly with misunderstanding and confusion, particularly when shopping. If I asked to buy two fish from the harbour I was given a bagful, and I often carried home a kilo of okra or some other unfamiliar vegetable without the slightest idea what I would do with it. Well-meaning shopkeepers, suspecting me of starving my husband with my meagre purchases, stuffed things into my basket. Greeks purchase food in alarming quantities, and anything less than a kilo is inconceivable to them. I felt intellectually inferior when they repeated what I'd just said but enunciated it more clearly, increasing the volume with each repetition – because, of course, I must also be deaf. Occasionally they made me a present of a bottle of wine 'for the artist', whom they seemed to perceive as long-suffering.

Within a couple of months I became expert at testing the feta cheese (made from ewes' milk). I knew my Kalamata olives from the Cretan variety and could tell a squid from an octopus, although I never mastered the art of *horta*-picking. *Horta* is the collective name for any type of edible green weed. All Greek women, regardless of age, scrutinise the roadside verges and fields for these greens which they cook as a side dish, much as we use potatoes. I was once given a long tour in the relentless sun (while the men drank beer) of a few acres of thorn-strewn land, my enthusiastic tutor expertly plucking at leafy things and repeating their names slowly for my benefit. I followed her lead and gathered what seemed an identical bunch. Every now and then she inspected my collection and yanked out offending stems, clicking her tongue in vexation and rolling her eyes heavenward. Obviously I was beyond help.

I soon learned that Greeks are snobs at heart: anyone who does not have to soil his hands to earn a living is regarded as both clever and respectable. Artists are particularly worthy and necessary in society because they have 'vision'. Everyone wanted to befriend my husband, for who but a man with a great mind could earn his living painting pictures rather than hoeing the olives?

At first the women watched me with interest and curiosity as I trekked down to the beach early in the mornings. They were not ashamed of staring and inexplicably I felt guilty. What must they think of me, I started asking myself. 'Why does this woman not cook for her man? Does she have no work to do?' I could feel their eyes boring through my beachbag and inspecting the contents. I began taking sneaky routes down to the sea.

Eventually I think I must have been given special dispensation as an artist's wife, for the women gave up on my *horta* lessons and grew tired of examining my beach paraphernalia. I concluded that seeing my washing hanging out to dry must have been enough to prove to them that I had at least one domestic skill and that that was all they could expect from this itinerant housewife.

The laundry was a daily struggle which I had to endure and win, if only to maintain some respectability in the community; I washed like a Trojan. I took a large bowl out into the yard and, barefoot and earnest, pounded away until the clothes were spotless. Washing clothes gave me a feeling of satisfaction that I'd never experienced at home, but when the sheets needed rinsing and wringing by hand my thoughts turned longingly to launderettes.

There are many customs in Crete and certain taboos. Women are never seen in the *kafeneon*, a peculiarly male establishment for drinking coffee and *raki* (a fiery clear alcohol made from fermented grapeskins). Unmarried women do not cut their hair and married women are rarely seen on a beach. Widows and widowers wear black for the rest of their lives, and many older men grow a beard after a family death. Babies are not named until they are a year old, and children live at home until they marry. Boys are spoiled and cossetted by their mothers and sisters alike, which no doubt accounts for the irritating habit many women have of fetching and carrying every small item their husbands require. I might have been considered a bad catch because I allowed my husband to reach his own ashtray and didn't feel the need to feed him titbits every few minutes. Although I spoke the language fairly well and my husband did not, some of the men waited for me to translate their entire conversation with him without even glancing at me. Such was his standing in the village that the men in the *kafeneon* accepted my presence there – indeed they were most welcoming, obviously indulging yet another eccentricity on the part of the foreigner.

I did not entirely master the art of Greek cuisine. Food is cooked very early in the morning, stewed for hours and left to go cold until night-time when it is reheated for the evening meal at around 9 p.m. I thought that this would lead to food poisoning in the intense heat, but the food was delicious and we were never ill. Most women cooked in one or two large pans, generally with gas or kerosene. Our kitchen had an excruciatingly slow electric ring but neither an oven or a grill, so naturally I developed a preference for salads. This is probably why I lost weight and felt twenty years younger. Since I also had an enviable sun-tan, I felt pretty good about myself. Without the constraints of work and pressure of time, the frantic rush of daily life disappeared. I had freedom to wander and time to ponder.

In the evenings the nearby market town was a lively and exciting venue from which to sell paintings. Albanian and Gypsy traders arrived for the season to sell everything from plastic chairs to sweetcorn and hairbraids. Several portrait painters worked in the Square and some nights we did well and sold many pictures, which gave us enough money for the rent and food, but on other evenings we stood there until midnight and sold nothing. Bitten to shreds by mosquitoes, we returned home either triumphant or deflated, it didn't matter which – because it was interesting, it was exciting, and it was a challenge.

We became good friends with a charming man called Christopholos who lived in a crumbling Venetian house high in the mountains. Although he had very little he gave us everything. He took us round the countryside in a small cart pulled behind his rotovator to weddings, festivals and picnics in beautiful locations. He cooked wonderful meals which we ate in his courtyard by the light of the moon, and whatever we did to repay him for his hospitality he returned tenfold. He often slept on our concrete yard because it was too hot indoors, but still rose at 5 a.m. to tend his fields of beans and artichokes. He was a wild and colourful character with a philosophy of enjoying one day at a time. Sometimes his humble unselfish lifestyle touched us on a raw nerve. By comparison we were wealthy and living a self-indulgent existence.

At festivals everyone joins in traditional dances and the *lyra* is played. This is a Cretan instrument similar to a violin but held on the player's knee. It produces an exotic wailing tone. We felt privileged to be part of these joyful occasions. There are special dances for the unmarried men and women. Through dance the men show their strength and bravery as *palikari* by performing boot-slapping leaps and complex footwork, while the young women whirl like spinning tops, faster and faster, to the accelerating high pitch of the *lyra*.

After six months my communication skills had improved but I was beginning to find the daily struggle to interpret for my husband unbearably tiring and longed to have a conversation in my own language, especially with another woman. The lack of rain caused me to dream of standing naked in a storm, only to wake and find myself soaked in sweat. I gazed at the arid mountain and thought of cool fern-clad waterfalls. Salad made my stomach churn. I wanted a piece of cheddar cheese. I could have *killed* for fish and chips. My thoughts turned to libraries, cinemas, and the luxury of a car. Although Cader Idris and Snowdon are molehills in comparison with the mountains of Crete, they became more and more appealing to me. At least they held no danger of treading on a scorpion or a snake, or of collapsing from heat exhaustion before I reached the top. The villagers were embroiled in petty squabbles, gossiping to me about one another, and I hated the rats that darted across the streets.

I was forced to admit I was missing my own country. There was a yearning in my heart that would not be still.

I weighed up one place against the other: clear blue skies, the scent of jasmine in the evening, turtles in the nearby lake – or the greyness of overcast skies. I compared the taste of drippingly delicious nectarines and figs picked straight from the tree to that of underripe fruit. But nothing could replace a spring morning walk after a light shower of rain, or a chat with a friend over coffee.

To my husband's astonishment I announced that I was resigning from the post he had created for me as Artist's Moll, packed my bags, waved farewell to our Cretan friends, and took the next flight home.

VI

I KNOW BECAUSE I WAS THERE

Many pieces in other chapters focus on aspects of the individual lives of the writers – individual experiences and details of their personal lives that were important to them and maybe only a few other people. This chapter, by contrast, brings together some accounts of events of local, national or international importance written by Welsh women who witnessed them, but they are not intended as 'history' or news reports; rather, they demonstrate the way in which public events can force their way into the consciousness of people preoccupied by other, more everyday, concerns, who find they have to react to these public events if only because of the way the public impacts on the private.

To all the writers in this chapter major dramatic events are a (usually unwelcome) interruption to real life. Gunfire in the Empress Market in Karachi temporarily disrupts shopping for the ingredients for an important dinner party; the eruption of Vesuvius makes the work of the army nurse more difficult; the coup d'état in Iraq restricts both the oil-company nurse's trip to the supermarket and her social life at expatriate clubs; the revolution in Portugal makes the teacher of English fear for her personal safety but also brings welcome time off work. Inevitably, all the writers bring their previous knowledge and assumptions to the events they describe: the notion that gunfire is an unusual occurrence; a knowledge of Roman history studied many years before; the assumption that 'Land of Hope and Glory' is a universally-understood signifier of defiant Britishness; the memory of personal danger at a time of political upheaval in another country. Their accounts are also inevitably partial in that the writers can describe only what they saw, heard or felt themselves while the main action was happening elsewhere, so that these accounts deal (to use the image in the piece on Empress Market) with some of the ripples on the water, not with the stone which created them.

These pieces throw up some striking contrasts and paradoxes. It is not the terrified Brit who keeps a stiff upper lip and talks about cricket and the weather when the bullets start flying in Empress Market but the Pakistani stall-holder (perhaps choosing traditional topics of British conversation to reassure her); an event in the present transforms the way the army nurse thinks about the past; the company nurse leaves her job in Somerset because the stress-levels it creates are too high, and goes to a situation which becomes not only far more stressful but potentially very dangerous; the dramatic and historic events of the revolution in Lisbon break into a day which the writer had expected to be like any other (there is even a contrast between the snarling feral cat on the Lisbon roof and the pampered pet of the writer's British friend).

Although the events themselves are very different the writers themselves are equally unprepared for them. All they can do is to react to them by making a comparison with something or someone from their home country (what Mam will think; school days in Tredegar; 'Land of Hope and Glory' on the record-player; the political system they grew up in) and then – literally or metaphorically – keep their heads down.

Incident at Empress Market

RONA LAYCOCK

The butcher sits at eye-level, arranging unidentifiable pieces of flesh; between his big toe and the next one he grasps a huge knife with stringy fibres hanging from it.

'Two pounds of beef, yes, *Memsahib*,' he says, and pulls a piece of beef to his side. Grasping the meat with both hands he uses the toe-clasped knife to carve off the approximate amount; then with a gap-toothed, swollen-cheeked grin he wraps the meat in yesterday's newspaper.

I pay him and turn away, avoiding the offal at my feet and the feral cats that spit in fury, to continue my shopping expedition. Before I get out of earshot I hear the butcher hawking and spitting profusely. I do not look back; my stomach is already heaving from the sights and sounds that surround me.

Out in the open-air market things are looking better: no rotting carcasses, no hungry cats, just stall after stall of fruit and vegetables being sniffed and prodded by the shoppers. Tall, handsome Pathan men wade through the crowds of their shorter southern relatives and twirl their moustaches as they pass each other in a graceful challenge. They are dressed in khaki with red turbans, and bandoliers of bullets decorate their chests. Their rifles catch on my basket, and I receive dazzling smiles of apology. I love this place; the bustle never stops and, although I am dressed in *shalwar khamees* like the local women, I am greeted as an honoured guest wherever I go.

I remember the first day I came to this market: I was horrified by the sight of chain-gangs being escorted by policemen who carried long poles which were used without mercy if someone stepped out of line, and by the mutilated stumps held out by lepers whose only chance of continued existence came from a successful day's begging. I saw it all, and promised myself I would never shop in the market again. It's funny how quickly you can adapt to just about anything: before long I had learned the ways of the country, learned not to judge it by the cultural standards I had brought with me, and found that shopping in the market had become an unremarkable part of my everyday life.

This particular day I am shopping for an important dinner party: the boss is coming, so all the stops are being pulled out. I have got the meat and now it is the turn of the vegetables. The stalls are piled high with colourful produce, and I take my time choosing exactly what I want. The melons look very good today, so I think that will take care of the starter. I am becoming loaded up with all sorts of goodies, and am beginning to feel the heat. Perhaps I should take this lot to the car and come back for the rest? Something buzzes past my ear and hits the wall behind the stallholder; he rushes forward, grabs me, and pushes me down behind his fruit as the crackle of gunfire disturbs the air.

'Sit here for while, *Memsahib*,' says my rescuer. 'Soon be over. Very hot today, don't you agree? I think perhaps the monsoon will come very soon indeed. Then we will have too much rain, flooding perhaps.'

I nod numbly; we are being shot at and he's talking about the weather. Then I ask, 'What's going on? Who's shooting?'

'Just a small argument between two men. Different tribes, you see. They come from the north – very different thing, not like here. Here we not shoot at each other. But no problem, all will be calm soon. No need to worry at all. Does your husband play cricket?'

I smile weakly and shake my head.

He continues as if unaware of the fusillade of bullets skittering off walls and paving slabs: 'Because you see there is a cricket match planned for tomorrow between team from British Consulate amd local team. I am very big fan of the cricket. Oh yes, very big fan indeed. We have very good national team – you too, I am thinking, but not quite as good as our team. Ah, I think all is calm now.'

The gunfire has ceased and as we emerge from our hiding-places (me shaking off a rat that seems to find my pink toes tempting), several Pathans are laughing and slapping each other on the back. I cannot see any bodies or wounded people; the incident has passed off, and the crowd has swallowed the adversaries as water swallows a stone. Only the ripples remain as we gather up our shopping and straighten our clothing.

'I will get boy to help you with your purchases,' announces the stall-holder. 'It has been nice to see you again, *Memsahib*. I am hoping your dinner-party goes well tonight.'

I reach the car and then have trouble controlling my knees and hands; it takes several attempts to get the key in the ignition. On the drive home I wonder if the incident would be a suitable topic of conversation for the dinner-party tonight. I know for sure that if I mentioned it to Mam she'd be on the next plane out to rescue me.

Vesuvius Lives!

FREDA BROADBANK

During World War II I was a sister in Queen Alexandra's Imperial Military Nursing Service Reserve and in 1944, after spending some time working in a military hospital in North Africa, I and my friend Mac were posted to 103 British General Hospital, which was housed in an Italian Army barracks in Nocera Inferiore, a village between Pompeii and Salerno. It was the first time I had been to Italy, and despite the war damage all around us I fell in love with the country.

A few days after our arrival, as we were driving with a group of friends to the Officers' Club in Castellamare, we noticed a great orange band running down one side of a nearby mountain. It looked ominous, but we didn't know what it might mean or what we could expect.

The next morning I was woken by Mac's cry of 'Look out of the window!' It was an amazing sight – the air was full of black ash falling. We found out afterwards that before the 'mountain' – Vesuvius – had erupted, the authorities had thought that the ash would be blown to the north of Naples and had evacuated all the villages in that area; instead it was blown to the south, and covered Nocera Inferiore. For more than a day it poured down on the hospital, and the authorities became afraid that the building's roof would collapse under the great weight. Any patient who could walk had to help in carrying the beds from the top storey down to the ground floor. The acrid smell of suphur was everywhere, and the air was full of ash and dust; we had to stop changing dressings because of the danger that the dust would infect the open wounds. After a few days, when the ash had stopped falling but had covered everything in layers several feet deep, soldiers from the Pioneer Corps came and shovelled it into great heaps, clearing pathways so that we could move about more easily once more.

Mac and I decided to visit Pompeii on our next day off, and hitched a lift there from the hospital. We had not realised before we got there that we would see the remains of a whole town, or how beautiful it had been: delicate frescoes of flowers, birds and plants, and scenes of the Gods and Cupid, their colouring so fresh and dainty that they might have been done yesterday, decorated some of the walls. There were streets with stepping-stones and the grooves made by chariot-wheels, wine-sellers' shops with large holes in the stone counters for wine jars, an arena, baths hot, cold and steam, and a crematorium. The symbolically-crooked 'Street of Immortality' left a vivid impression on me of the ingenuity of the human mind and the fragility of human life in comparison with the ferocity of nature which we had just witnessed. As we left the site, small boys tried to sell us phials of Vesuvian ash; since we had almost been buried by the stuff we felt that we had already seen more than enough of it, and did not need souvenirs to remind us of our recent experiences. Seeing the eruption of Vesuvius and the place we lived in covered (although only temporarily) by a pall of ash made us feel that there was a bond between us and the people who had lived in Pompeii, as if we were colleagues who knew part of their story at first hand because of the experiences we shared with them, not tourists who came to gawp at them and their homes as if they were curiosities.

Shortly afterwards we spent a week's leave in Rome, and were lucky enough to get a lift there in a staff car. We had a wonderfully luxurious journey along the Via Appia – one of the greatest straight roads in the Roman Empire, built for the Imperial armies to march along. Long stretches of it were lined with trees; in one place there were oleanders, covered in beautiful pink blossom. By late afternoon our road had reached the coast, so we stopped for a swim and tea. The sand was clean – no dust from volcanoes here – and the sea was clear and blue. It was nearly dark by the time we were nearing Rome; the sun was setting in a blaze of diffuse golden light which became a clear red ball before it finally sank beneath the horizon, and its reflection lay along the Pontine Marshes I remembered reading about in my schooldays. We finally entered Rome by moonlight.

At school in Tredegar we used to plod slowly and laboriously through Caesar's *De Bella Gallica* (On the Gallic Wars), a book that had seemed a world away in time and place from our own teenage lives; how different it would have been if I'd had a chance to see then the places I was reading about in Roman History classes. Now at last I'd seen the very mountains and marshes and travelled on the plains and roads that he had written about, and some of the people I'd met and seen must have been descended from his soldiers. I thought of the people in Pompeii who had seen black ash falling from the sky as I had, and who, centuries before me, had walked as I had down the crooked Street of Immortality. History suddenly became a living thing to me, and the stones of the past were real and heavy in my hand.

Sheep May Safely Graze

CYNTHIA J. HARRIS

A flock of cautious sheep moved slowly past, looking for food; it was hard to believe that they would find any in that stony wasteland. Occasionally one would stop to tease at a tuft of coarse grass, but such morsels were few and far between and contained little nourishment – and yet this was a landscape in which sheep had safely grazed for hundreds of years. The sheep were scrawny and lethargic, unlike the sheep which grew fat on the lush green grass of the Welsh hillsides I knew. Their shepherd urged them on towards the more fertile hills which lay to the north. He was dressed as desert dwellers had dressed for centuries, right back to the Mesopotamia of biblical times – indeed, this might have been a scene from biblical times but for the twelve-foot high chain-link fence which separated the hospital compound from the surrounding desert.

National borders in the area had been redefined, most recently by European diplomats who had created the kingdom of Iraq. Iraq was now an oil-rich country, and but for the oil the fence in the desert would not have been there; it kept intruders – including the sheep – out of the hospital compound. But for the oil, the eternal fires and the fiery furnace (an enormous cleft in a rock which gushed angry flames) would not have been there: and but for the oil, neither would I.

*   *   *

I had been happy working as a midwife in Somerset but our team all too often had only two midwives instead of four, and our stress levels mounted. I told myself there must be an easier way to earn a living and, in 1957, answered an advertisement for a general-duties nursing sister in Kirkuk, Iraq. I had only the vaguest idea where Iraq was and had never heard of Kirkuk.

I was to work for the next two years at the Iraq Petroleum Company hospital, and my 'home' would be the sisters' mess. There was a swimming-pool, cinema and super-market in the main compound, with open-air dancing on Friday nights. The hospital was well equipped – light, airy, air-conditioned – and well staffed: as well as the British nursing sisters there were Iraqi sisters who hd trained in the UK and orderlies, most of whom had worked there for several years and had considerable experience and expertise. The work was less arduous than I had been used to, and after my experiences as a midwife the hours were a dream. There were three wards: one for daily-paid unskilled and semi-skilled employees, one for monthly-paid and salaried staff and their dependants, and one for female employees and dependants of monthly-paid and salaried employees.

Most company employees were relatively young and therefore healthy; there were no wards full of men strug-gling to breathe after a lifetime working in the Welsh pits. Cuts, fractures, hernias and appendicitis were common surgical conditions; dysentery and parasitic infestation accounted for the majority of medical patients; hookworm infestation was widespread and caused severe anaemia, the cause of many a child's death.

A well-equipped maternity ward catered for the needs of expatriate wives and the wives of Iraqi senior staff, although Iraqi women traditionally delivered at home; the admission of a young Iraqi girl in the throes of a miscarriage was an unprecedented event. She was accompanied by a female friend, but shortly after she was admitted her parents arrived, refused to believe she was suffering from hookworm infestation and took her away. She was unmarried and a Muslim; her lover was a Christian. She had dishonoured her family on both counts, and not to punish her would be an added disgrace; death alone would preserve the family honour. It occurred to me that in some Western societies (including Wales) where abortion was illegal at the time, fear of disgracing the family name led many young girls to submit to the brutality of a backstreet abortionist by whose hand she might end up just as dead as if her father or brother had killed her. Intolerance is intolerance.

At about the same time a man was convicted of murdering his wife; I don't remember his motive, but I know he was condemned to death. He appealed on the grounds that if he was put to death there would be no one to look after his children, and his sentence was quashed. At first this seemed to be blatant injustice, but then I asked myself, who *would* have looked after his children? There were no social services to help, or children's homes.

But it wasn't all work. To British expatriates who had experienced the restrictions and austerities of World War II and post-war years, our life in Iraq was luxurious by comparison. The company provided high-quality accommodation which was well equipped, fully air-conditioned and rent-free, with no electricity bills or rates to pay. There were bungalows for families and communal messes for single workers or those unaccompanied by their spouses, good sports facilities and a well-stocked library. Mindful of the moral welfare of their employees, the company had entrusted the task of censoring new books to the Anglican canon. On one occasion he authorised the purchase of a book without checking on its subject-matter: its title was *Cast the First Stone*, and since this was a quotation from the Bible he was certain the book would be suitable. When it arrived it turned out to be an academic investigation of the sociology of prostitution, and was withdrawn from circulation before it even got through the library door.

Not only Christmas and New Year were celebrated but also national saints' days: for the first time since I was at school I celebrated St. David's Day. We hospital sisters also had our own party in June; the one in early June 1958 was particularly memorable, not only because we roasted two whole sheep and made salad for 120 people, but for the amount of alcohol our guests consumed.

It turned out to be not only memorable but the last party of all. On the morning of 11th July a colleague and I went to the supermarket in the hospital compound as usual, but after ten minutes the manager told us that a curfew was just about to begin and we would have to leave; we protested that we hadn't finished our shopping, but he was politely adamant. Back at the Mess, we phoned friends and tried to find out what had happened, but no one seemed to know why the curfew had been imposed; it permitted employees to travel between their homes and places of work but confined their dependants to their homes. It was rapidly replaced by a dawn-to-dusk curfew. International borders were closed, all planes were grounded, and postal and telephone services were suspended; we couldn't leave and we couldn't tell our relatives in Britain that we were safe. Rumours were rife, but for many days they were only rumours. Then the death of the young King Feisal was confirmed, but the circumstances of his death were unclear: nobody wanted to believe that he had been assassinated. There had been no hint of dissent that we were aware of, no public anti-royalist demonstrations; most Iraqis appeared to us to be pro-British and patriotic royalists. Rumours began to circulate that all members of the royal family who had been at the palace that night had been assassinated. The dusk-to-dawn curfew remained in force and the company security guards, such as the one who manned the entrance to our compound, were augmented by armed military patrols.

Airwaves were something that could not be controlled, however, and we eventually learned the truth via the BBC World Service. The revolutionaries had been very thorough. Not only had members of the royal family living in Iraq been murdered but also every member of the royal family world-wide; nobody who might one day retaliate and lay claim to the throne of Iraq was spared. Overnight the country became a republic under the military control of Abdul Karim Kassim.

We received assurances that foreign nationals were in no danger and that the new regime had no quarrel with the company. This was not surprising, as the Iraqi economy was heavily dependent on oil revenues and it was in the country's best interests that production should continue uninterrupted. We were repeatedly assured that we had no need to worry as long as we complied with the orders of the new regime. Machine-gun posts were set up around the oil-fields, although it was never clear whether this was to keep us in or intruders out.

It was amazing how quickly people adapted to this new way of life, although there were some who regarded the restrictions as a challenge. In the hospital compound we were fortunate because of the close proximity of our neighbours and, with the arrogance of youth and a belief in our own immortality, those of us who got bored with spending every evening looking at our own four walls broke out. My best friends lived on the other side of the compound, and more than a hundred yards separated us; the area between us was sparsely planted with oleander and palm trees. We would hide behind a palm frond and then dart from oleander to palm tree in an attempt to evade the sentry. He probably thought we were too crazy to bother about; we were never challenged, although I can't believe we were never seen.

The Iraqi newspapers which had proclaimed the new republic published pictures showing the opulence of the royal palaces alongside pictures of the poorest of peasant dwellings; the people of Iraq were told that the royal wealth now belonged to them. Royalists and alleged royalists were sought out or betrayed and then arrested; brothers turned against brothers and fathers against sons. Many sought sanctuary in the hospital, presenting with chest pains which could have been heart attacks. There were many betrayals in Kirkuk at that time, but no reports of street-fighting. From Mosul, however – further north – news filtered through of fighting between Kurds and the army of the new republic, and of indescribable atrocities. Bodies were ripped apart, and lamp-posts became gallows.

After a few weeks we were put under a curfew which confined us to the compound from 10.30 p.m. until dawn; this was believed to be a step nearer normality. After six weeks the borders were reopened and the first civil aircraft was allowed to leave from Kirkuk, an American charter flight for dependants of Americans working in and around the city. The first oil company charter flight brought back employees and some families whose stay in Britain had been unexpectedly extended, and took back those employees and their families whose leave had been postponed because of the crisis. When the postal service was eventually restored each employee was allowed to send one letter only, and this was censored. One of the hospital sisters came from the Outer Hebrides and her first language was Scots Gaelic; her mother understood nothing else. Naturally her letter to her mother was written in Gaelic but the Iraqi security service had no Gaelic-speaking interpreter; she was ordered to write the letter in English. She explained coldly that she was her mother's only child and her mother understood only Gaelic. The letter went uncensored.

We continued to believe that the Iraqis bore the British no ill-will until the British Consul in Kirkuk was expelled without warning; his family had already left and he was given only days to follow them. Cocooned as we were in the oil company compound we never imagined that we might need his services and at first his departure seemed unimportant.

Gradually, however, we became aware that things were changing. For example, senior Iraqi employees had always had automatic membership of the oil company club and although those who used it were welcomed, very few had ever done so. In the early days of the republic one of these was arrested at the club, and after this they were noticeable by their absence; it is possible that their membership of what was essentially a British club was felt to call into question their loyalty to the new regime. From January 1st 1959, however, the atmosphere changed. There was a positive invasion of the club by men who were merely making a point; our friendly overtures to them were spurned. Even some of the club waiters and barmen became somewhat hostile, and it was difficult not to feel intimidated. To avoid unpleasantness some expatriates began using the golf club, which was a private club and therefore open to (British) members and their guests only. The armed guards whom we had cheerfully dodged during curfew hours in the early days became increasingly aggressive and missed no opportunity to exert their authority. We could no longer be sure of anyone's friendship, except perhaps the Kurds, and even they were wary of any show of friendliness in public.

Perhaps we had been too complacent, too sure that the troubles did not concern us. Perhaps we were too stubborn to realise that the easier early days had been merely a period of consolidation, when arms could be amassed, new troops recruited and the new army trained. One morning our private compound was invaded by lorry-loads of soldiers waving palm-fronds and shouting, 'Abdul Karim Kassim!' It was a beautiful spring morning; the daffodils had been coaxed into bloom and the violets were a riot of royal purple. The invasion of our compound was an infringement of our privacy which we could not tolerate: some form of retaliation was vital, and we felt we knew the very thing. We put on a record, turned up the volume and flung wide the windows, but the strains of *Land of Hope and Glory* played by full orchestra only reverberated through the bungalow and made no impression at all on the chanting revolutionaries outside. In retrospect this was probably just as well.

I gradually realised the futility of refusing to accept that the situation was becoming untenable. I was due some home leave and everyone, including my Iraqi friends, urged me not to come back. My future was undecided and ostensibly I was saying *au revoir* and not goodbye, but I suppose I knew deep down that I was saying farewell for ever to many of my friends.

I thought at the time that when the country became stable, when the Iraqi people no longer lived in fear, I would return. Almost half a century has passed, and too many people in Iraq still live in fear. I have never returned. I wonder, do the sheep still safely graze in the stony wasteland?

April in Portugal

GWYNETH TYSON ROBERTS

I woke in the early hours of the morning with a sense that something somewhere was wrong: the whole flat seemed to be shaking gently. The shaking continued as I moved closer to full consciousness; this was getting serious. I got out of bed, walked to the door, and put both hands flat against the wall next to the lintel. Through my palms I could feel a slight vibration and another, slower, shaking movement.

That decided things: it must be an earthquake. Since I lived on the top – fifth – floor there seemed no point in trying to make my way downstairs; if the building was going to collapse shortly I didn't want to be halfway down the stairs when it happened and have the upper storeys fall on top of me. I decided to stay where I was in the frame of the flat's main doorway so that if the building collapsed I would descend gracefully on top of the rubble rather than underneath it (I was completely ignorant of the way earthquakes work). I stood there, listening to the sound of cars in the street outside blaring their horns, and shouting voices and running feet from the floors of the building below me, for about ten minutes. By that time the shouting had stopped and the excitement seemed to be over.

My first earthquake, I thought. I'd had a fire in my flat some months before and I'd been in a country at war when I was working in Iraq several years earlier, and now here was something else to cross off my list. I made coffee, went back to bed and wondered if we'd get the day off work.

I lived in an old building in Lisbon. My flat was immediately under the steeply-pitched roof and overlooked the grounds of the Prime Minister's official residence, which was surrounded by two high walls with a walkway between them and guard-posts at intervals. Three or four guards were usually visible; in the summer they sat around in unbuttoned uniform jackets, smoking and playing cards; in the winter they walked up and down and around in small circles, stamping their feet to keep warm, their faces pinched in the cold and damp.

A crazed ginger cat would occasionally appear on the roof snarling and spitting, presumably living the rest of the time in the other flat on the fifth floor although the occupants became vague when asked about it. Sometimes it would hurl itself at one of my windows, hissing menacingly and baring its teeth (this was particularly unnerving in the early hours of the morning when I'd just come back from a good party). It would disappear for weeks, sometimes months, at a time and I would forget all about it, so that its ferocious reappearance would be a shock as well as an intimidation. Friends sometimes suggested I should cultivate it by offering tasty morsels of fish and meat 'to win its confidence', but its lack of trust in me was the least of my concerns: it looked like the sort of cat that filed its teeth into sharp points. Occasionally I would snarl back at it through the safely-bolted window; it seemed to find this reassuring.

As teachers of English at the British Institute we had been warned on arrival in Portugal never to mention politics or religion in class or allow others to mention them, but since I had no interest in either subject this was no hardship. Knowing it was likely that each of my classes contained a spy for the secret police merely gave my everyday work an enjoyable frisson, with the additional interest of trying to work out exactly who the spy was (in some classes, rumour had it, a second spy would be installed to spy on the first one). Several foreign teachers of English had lived in my flat in the past, which apparently made it more likely that the phone was regularly tapped; when we remembered about it my friends and I would deliberately fill our phone conversations with 'cryptic' references and allusions in order to confuse any secret listener, so that possible surveillance became a joke. I floated through my life there only vaguely aware of the crushing of dissent, of the political, social and economic strains caused by the wars in Portugal's African colonies, and hardly thought of the human cost until one day I heard from a casual remark that an ex-student of mine had been reported killed in the war in Angola. He'd been in one of my advanced classes the previous year, and I remembered him well: he was engaging, clever and slapdash, with a wicked sense of humour, and the news of his death was shockingly difficult to take in. I started to say, 'But—' and then realised that all the ways I might have ended the sentence ('But he was so full of life.' 'But I didn't even know he'd been called up.' 'But no one told me he was fighting in Angola.') were insultingly trivial and fatuous. A few evenings later, sitting on a friend's balcony and having a long cool drink as the sun went down, I noticed an open army lorry making its way through the traffic in the street below, the two cheap-looking military-issue coffins in the back jolting around as the driver accelerated over the cobbles, and felt a sudden sharp sense of human loss; and then the moment passed, and normal life resumed.

One weekday morning in late April 1974 I got up, turned on the radio for the usual aural wallpaper of news headlines, commercials and pop music, and gradually became aware that something different was happening: the voices were new, excited, and a little nervous, and the information coming in quick unco-ordinated bursts was all about the armed forces. Apparently there was a revolution in progress.

I phoned friends, other friends phoned me; no one seemed to know exactly what was going on or how much, after so many years of news being controlled, we could trust what we heard on the radio. After an hour or so, frustrated at not having a clear picture of events (and also finding it difficult to believe that something so huge and historic was happening without warning on a day that had seemed like any other) I went out to see what was going on in my neighbourhood.

The answer seemed to be 'not much'. Shops and offices were all closed, buses and trams had apparently stopped running and there were no taxis. I was glad to see that the British Institute building was firmly closed: work was clearly out of the question. Occasionally a car would race down the middle of the street, speeding away from the centre of the city; there were almost no pedestrians. Lorry-loads of soldiers blocked access to the National Assembly building a couple of hundred yards from my block of flats in the direction of the river.

I climbed back up the stairs to my flat. Something had clearly started, whatever it might turn out to be, and I began to feel afraid. I had been in Baghdad seven years before at the time of the 'six-day' Arab-Israeli war, when Iraqis were being told that RAF planes were flying in support of Israel, and what had alarmed me then was less the experience of being threatened and spat at in the street than the knowledge of my complete helplessness in the face of frightening and dangerous events. It occurred to me

belatedly that living close to the National Assembly building *and* to the Prime Minister's official residence could
have major disadvantages: if I left the flat and street-
fighting broke out around the two official buildings it
might be impossible to get back, while if they were targeted
by artillery with less than perfect aim my block of flats
might be right in the line of fire (I knew nothing about
urban warfare either).

I made more phone calls. I listened to the radio. Rumours
of what the President and the Prime Minister were doing
seemed to change every few minutes. They had gone to an
airforce base outside Lisbon, they had taken refuge in an
underground bunker, they had just arrived at the Carmo
barracks in central Lisbon believing that no one would fire
at them there for fear of civilian casualties, they had fled to
the north, they had slipped over the border into Spain (the
ultimate betrayal). Late in the morning I got a phone call
from a middle-aged British woman I'd known slightly for a
couple of years; she had studied music in Leipzig in the
1930s, worked first as a naval draughtswoman and later as
an antiques dealer in Canada, and was now in Lisbon
studying musical composition and complaining about her
professor's choice of girl-friends. She lived in one of the
villages 'up the line' (near the local railway line from
Lisbon to Cascais and Estoril), and she was phoning me
now because she had a serious problem: no fish for her cat.
She had, she said, gone to her local market that morning to
get a nice piece of fish for Timmy's dinner only to discover
that everywhere was closed with the ridiculous excuse that
a revolution was under way, so would I just buy some fish
in Lisbon and take it out to her?

I explained that all shops and markets in Lisbon – not
only in my area but, according to the radio, throughout the
city – were shut and barred and that even if I'd had a

fridgeful of fish I'd have been unable to get it to her: she lived about ten miles away, I had no car, and there were no buses, trains, trams or taxis. This, as far as she was concerned, was completely irrelevant; she kept trying to persuade me to magic some fish into existence ('Even a *small* piece would do for the time being, and Timmy's such a lovely cat'), and at one point held her telephone receiver close to the animal's mouth in the hope that hearing the hungry feline wails would soften my hard heart. Eventually she rang off, angry with me and convinced that I wasn't *making enough of an effort*; I was so heartened by the ludicrousness of the conversation that I stopped being afraid and began to feel cheerful again.

In the afternoon I ventured out to join some friends in the crowd outside the Carmo barracks, where it now seemed that the President and Prime Minister really had taken refuge. There were shouts and jeers at both of them but the prevailing atmosphere in the crowd was of near-disbelief that this could be happening, which at moments swung into a sudden marvelling delight at the thought that if this *could* happen then anything was possible. A few people were carrying red carnations.

More and more red carnations filled the streets in the days that followed; people carried them, pinned them to their clothes and put them down the barrels of the rifles of the soldiers guarding major security points and installations. The soldiers started to relax a little. After a few days when it felt as if the country was holding its breath, it became clear that none of the important and influential units of the armed forces was prepared to stand on its own to fight for the old regime; the revolution was almost bloodless. The President (of whom it was literally true that God – 'Deus', in this case – was his middle name) was rumoured to have been put in prison, to have fled to Franco in Spain, and to have escaped to Brazil in a submarine. It eventually became clear that wherever he was, he had gone.

A few days after 25th April I passed the headquarters of the secret police. The building had been ransacked, and the pavements and roadway were covered by shattered window-panes and thousands of pieces of white paper from torn-up files that fluttered in the wind like rough fragments of confetti. The son of the optician in the block opposite mine was outed as a neighbourhood spy for the secret police; a huge crowd gathered in the street to see him taken out at gunpoint through his father's shop and driven off in the back of an army lorry under heavy guard.

Banners hung across streets, posters and painted slogans suddenly appeared on every wall, everyone seemed to be wearing badges showing their political affiliation, and all the badges had red carnations. New types of graffiti appeared and the words 'Clean me', traditionally scrawled dis-dainfully in the dust on the dirty windscreens of parked cars, now became 'Clean me, you fascist pig'. A wide range of social projects began: the son of one of my colleagues joined a group that started to cultivate disused and neglected land – part of the vast estates of wealthy aristocratic landowners – for the benefit of local people. (Another of my colleagues, originally from a land-owning family, was appalled: 'They've taken some of the land of the Duke of Leixões? The *Duke of Leixões?* But he's such a charming man, and *so* fond of music!') The word *comité* suddenly appeared everywhere, as did the verb *boicotar* (meaning 'to campaign vigorously against'). Political exiles came back, while some people who had been closely connected with the old regime left the country suddenly, often with banknotes and jewellery in their underwear in an attempt to beat the new restrictions on exporting valuables. Political parties formed, faded, revived, changed, split, re-formed and split again: Revolutionary, Democratic, Socialist, Anarchist, Marxist, Leninist, Trotskyite, Stalinist, Maoist. Especially in the north a few rightwing groupings emerged, often monarchist or with the backing of the Church; one proud father was said to have hedged his bets by registering his new-born son's name as 'Stalin de Jesus'.

Suddenly everything seemed full of possibilities and there was a sense of having a chance to remake the country; the planned elections were for the body which would draw up a new Constitution. Writers no longer felt they had to avoid political issues or write in code. Films which had been banned for a couple of generations, including classics of the Russian cinema, were shown to large and enthusiatic audiences. One of my most inspiring memories of the time was watching *The Battleship Potemkin* in a Lisbon cinema where the audience was largely composed of Portuguese sailors for whom the film's depiction of the part played by sailors in the beginnings of the Russian revolution had a special and powerful meaning. Everything seemed clearer and brighter.

The following months were full of more political manoeuvering; there were protests, conspiracies and rumours of a counter-coup and several counter-counter-coups. I found that the provenance of the sentries on the garden wall of the Prime Minister's residence provided a useful barometer of political volatility: if they were from ordinary infantry regiments, things were quiet; if they were paratroopers, trouble was possible; if they were marines, a crisis was imminent. The rumour machine was always busy – a friend of a friend had always just heard from an umimpeachable source the true story behind the latest near-crisis – but gradually it became clear that the change was permanent.

I had lived through a revolution, and could cross another item off my imaginary list.

At the same time I knew that however much I supported the changes, I stood apart from them: it wasn't *my* country's institutions that were being remade, *my* country's future that was being decided. The idea that the changes I had seen could happen in other countries too, that the political structure of a society – including the one I grew up in – was not an unchangeable 'given' but could be rethought and remade, took some time to work its way through my unpoliticised brain. The revolution was a revelation.

After a long absence the ginger cat suddenly reappeared on the roof. Its teeth were as vicious as ever.

VII

OPPOSITE ENDS OF THE SPECTRUM

In the second half of the twentieth century international travel became easier, quicker and cheaper, and the pieces in this book reflect this. The difficulty and expense of travel before the beginning of the twentieth century meant that it was a relatively unusual experience, especially for working-class women, and the two passages which follow are included to suggest some of the extremes of this experience for Welsh women travelling and living abroad before 1900.

Betsy Cadwaladyr, independent, decisive and never reluctant to say exactly what she thought about anyone or anything, would probably have stood out by sheer force of personality in any age; by contrast, Elizabeth Prichard, one of the earliest settlers of Y Wladfa Gymreig – the Welsh settlement in Patagonia – is shown as reacting to events rather than making them happen, and as dependent on others for security as well as physical and economic survival. It is important to remember that the lives of the great majority of Welsh women abroad in the nineteenth (and earlier) centuries would have been much closer to hers than to that of the remarkable Betsy Cadwaladyr.

There is a further telling contrast in the way their stories have come down to us. Betsy Cadwaladyr speaks directly to us in her own words – her autobiography, by Jane Williams (Ysgafell), is an impressive early example of oral history – while we know of Elizabeth Prichard's life not only through the words of (male) others, but through documents that survived by the merest chance. Her story can stand as a memorial to the thousands of Welsh women of the past who went to settle abroad, often in hardship, poverty, inhospitable terrain, difficulties and dangers, and who now are forgotten because they did not have a voice of their own.

'I Must See Something More of the World'

BETSY CADWALADYR

Betsy Cadwaladyr's other name was Elizabeth Davis; she was the daughter of Judith Erasmus and Dafydd Cadwaladyr (Davis), a preacher well-known in his day from one of the groups within Calvinistic Methodism (the Countess of Huntingdon's Connexion). She grew up in Wales as Betsy Cadwaladyr but later used the official version of her name because the English people she was then living among found it easier to pronounce. She says she was probably born around 1795 near Bala, Merionydd (apparently the relevant pages of the family Bible were torn out), and was one of the youngest of sixteen brothers and sisters. When she was five her much-loved mother died and after this she was brought up by one of her older sisters whom she disliked intensely. At the age of nine she ran away to Bala and was taken in by the family of her father's landlord, who taught her reading, writing and English as well as housework, needlework, baking and laundry work. After five years she agreed to stay with them for another year as a household servant, but: 'In the course of the following Sunday night a sudden thought occurred to me that I was not to stay there any longer and that I must see something more of the world', so she ran away – first to her astonished aunt in Chester and then (using the money her aunt had given her to travel home) to Liverpool, where she got a job as a housemaid and travelled with her employers to France, Spain, Belgium, Italy and the West Indies as well as within Britain. She then took a job as maid to the wife of a merchant ship's captain who accompanied her husband on his voyages, and at this point her travels really began; the ship (the Denmark Hill*) visited Greece, Egypt, South Africa, Australia and Tasmania, New Zealand, Singapore, India, China, Hawaii, Peru, Argentina and Brazil. She travelled for two days inland from Singapore on the back of an elephant in the company of three Burmese noblewomen with whom she was unable to communicate except by smiling and pointing, saw a British naval officer stabbed to death next to her in Rio de Janeiro, performed the sleepwalking scene from* Macbeth *in Calcutta (Kolkut) and was pursued halfway round the world by a Portuguese merchant who said his father was 'brother to King John the Eighth of Portugal' and who had a habit of suddenly appearing in front of her when she least expected it, giving her significant glances and sighing ostentatiously. On her travels she met with several attempted rapes, several more attempted seductions and many offers of marriage; she became engaged several times, but the prospect of committing herself to a man seems to have had the same effect on her as committing herself to a job, and she immediately felt she had to run in the opposite direction.*

The Autobiography of Elizabeth Davis – Betsy Cadwaladyr: A Balaclava Nurse, *by Jane Williams (Ysgafell), from which these abridged extracts are taken, was first published in 1857 and reissued by Honno in 1987. Her opportunity to visit Canton came when the merchant ship docked there during a voyage which called at Calcutta, Sri Lanka, Mauritius, Madras, Singapore and Sydney.*

From Mauritius we sailed to Siam, and loaded there with goods for Madras. There we loaded a general cargo, with fine woods and ivory for Canton. On reaching that city we anchored in Cock Lane to discharge the cargo, and then went up to the East India Company's Factory and loaded the ship with tea. The foreman there was an old Chinaman, who had been thirty years in the Factory. He used often to come on board the *Denmark Hill* for a meal of beef and biscuit and grog, and I made a joke of asking him to take me to see the city. One day I told him that I would give him no more beef or grog until he took me. I thought the thing impossible, and only said it to tease him. The old man looked very hard at me, as much as to say, 'Are you in earnest?' He went on shore and I thought no more about it. He spoke English very well.

The next morning, about nine o'clock, I was very much surprised to see a grand native boat come alongside our ship. This great boat was of all the colours of the rainbow, with the Union Jack and the Company's flag flying together at the stern. The rowers were ten Chinamen dressed all in white, with green sashes. The boatswain wore a pink robe with a red sash, and had a white and green cap on his head with a very large green and red feather. They all wore satin slippers with wooden soles to them and very narrow turned-up toes.

At the same time the old foreman, Fa Pooh, came on board the *Denmark Hill* from the Factory, bringing a passport in his hand for my mistress and me to see the city. She was afraid and would not go, but I would not lose such a chance, so I dressed myself up in a pink gingham dress and went alone in the barge in the care of the little boatswain. Neither he nor any of the crew could speak English, and when I talked English to them they stared foolishly at me, but when I spoke Welsh to them they pointed out the different places that came in sight as we went along the river, and I never will believe but that they knew what I said.

They took me as near as the barge could go to the gates of Canton, and I landed and had to take care afterwards of myself. Fa Pooh had told me what I was to do. I gave in my passport, expecting that it would be looked at and returned to me, but instead of that I was kept waiting so long that I grew very uneasy, for the Tartar sentinels were staring fiercely at me all the time. The gatekeeper at last gave me a new passport, which he had been writing out while I stood there. The same thing was done at all the other gates which I passed through that day, I think I had twelve passports in going through the city.

Being let in, I wandered about and saw a great many craftsmen at all sorts of works. Some were weaving, others making cabinets, others turning with a lathe. Every one was busy that I saw, and they were all gentle and civil in their manner towards me, but they eyed me, I thought, as if they mis-doubted me; there was not one woman among them. I felt uneasy, and was sorry that I had come. None of them uttered a word to me, nor did I speak to them.

Not knowing where I went, I got at length to the Royal Square, where I found a great number of women all very industrious and working in groups at all kinds of things; some were at embroidery, some were weaving silk, some turning ivory or making fans. I think there were five hundred there. They all seemed by their manner to be ladies. They were beautiful creatures, very fair with a delicate pink colour in their cheeks; I do not know whether it was paint or not. Their eyes were too small to have life enough in them. They were very silent, but looked pleased at me. I was told afterwards that this was the Emperor's harem.

I began to talk Welsh to them, and their leader, who seemed to act as foreman in their work, took me round, upstairs and downstairs, and showed me everything. I think she understood what I said. I am sure there is some connection between the Welsh and Chinese languages.

The old princess looked at my dress and smiled and patted my cheek, and we were very good friends. I stayed some hours with these kind ladies and when I was coming away the old princess fetched a small parcel folded up in a China silk-gauge handkerchief. I was very thankful for her kindness and I tried to shake hands with her, saying '*Diolch yn fawr i chwi*,' and making a curtsey. She kissed my hand and I went away.

I did not know where I was going, and got into a gallery and passed along it for some distance. It skirted the Royal Square, but because all ways seemed the same to me I stopped short at a door in it and passed into the longest room I ever beheld in my life. The walls were bare and there was no furniture except for two images with a great deal of Chinese writing around them. In the further end of the room several men were sitting together in a group upon the ground.

I scarcely had time to notice these particulars when a gentleman came rushing after me saying, 'For God's sake, don't go there! It's as much as your life is worth!' I was frightened and asked, 'What have I done?' He answered, 'Don't you know where you are? Down on your knees! And stop like that until I tell you!' I sat down on the floor and he fell on his knees and raised his joined hands as if he was praying.

One of the men from the other end of the room now got up. He wore a long robe glittering with precious stones and had in his hand a sceptre about three yards long with a sort of crown on the top of it. With that he came towards us and measured three times its length from the spot where the gentleman (Mr Cruikshanks, I found out later) knelt. Mr Cruikshanks then walked that distance on his knees, with his hands lifted up as if in prayer. The man measured a second distance, and Mr Cruikshanks passed it in the same way. When he reached the group, they made him sit down cross-legged. By and by he was brought back again with the same ceremonies and told me that he had explained about me and that I was to do everything just as he had done it. I found great difficulty in getting along, for my petticoats hindered me and I was obliged to tuck the princess's parcel across the back of my legs. When I got to the group of gentlemen I sat down cross-legged as Mr Cruikshanks had done. They all looked at me and laughed; the youngest and most plainly-dressed of them handed me a pipe. I never thought that they could intend me to smoke it, but supposed they wished me to see how pretty it was, so I took it all to pieces and looked at it bit by bit, and gave the biggest part back to the young Emperor who had passed it to me. At this they were more amused than ever and laughed very heartily.

All went well until it wa time to go; the man measured out the distance with his sceptre again and I tried to imitate the way Mr Cuikshanks had walked backwards upon his knees with his hands together. I scrambled and crawled somehow or other along the first distance but when the chamberlain measured the next I lost all patience, for the group all shrieked out and the old man shook me with angry looks for not going in the right posture, so I suddenly started to my feet and ran out of the room face-foremost and down a flight of many hundred marble steps and into a fine chapel and through it to the riverbank. I could go no further in that direction, so I recrossed the chapel; it was inlaid with dazzling stones, and there were no idols in it.

In going up the marble steps I met Mr Cruikshanks coming towards me. He said it was a mercy he had seen me, or I should never have come out of that room alive. The young Emperor had only arrived in Canton the day before, and was sitting in council when I went in upon him.

About eight o'clock in the evening I got safe back to the ship. I opened the princess's parcel, and found in it a fine camel's-hair dress, of a yellow and white striped pattern, the white being like open needlework. It had hanging sleeves and strings with tassels to draw it into shape. I thought it was too short for me, so I gave it to my mistress who asked me for it. I heard afterwards that she was offered eighty pounds for it.

After leaving the employment of the captain's wife she became a housekeeper in London, invested and lost her earnings in a dubious house-purchase scheme that went wrong, was cheated by her employer's family of a substantial legacy in his will, and in her late fifties earned her living as a nurse in London, lodging with her sister Bridget. In the summer of 1853 Russia's claim to protect not only the Holy Places in Jerusalem but also Christians living within the Ottoman Empire sparked a military confrontation with Britain and France: on 20th September 1854 British and French armies defeated a Russian force at the Battle of the Alma.

After having been abroad I always liked to know what was going on in the world, and this curiosity made me an eager reader of the newspapers. Sitting one evening with my sister Bridget, I read in one of them an account of the battle of the Alma.

'Oh,' I said, 'if I had wings, would I not go!'

'What,' said Bridget, 'go to be a soldier? Well, I can believe anything if you have changed your mind about them.'

I did not want to be a soldier but to see what was going on, and to take care of the wounded. Then again, I read of Miss Nightingale preparing to take out nurses. I did not like the name of Nightingale. When I first hear a name I am very apt by my feeling to know whether I shall like the person who bears it.

I determined that I would try to go to the Crimea. I dressed myself and set off to the solicitor named in the newspaper. When I got there I thought I was in a nunnery – I saw so many women and only one man. He was the Rev. Mr Shepherd: he asked my history and occupation and said that if I had applied to him two or three days before I could have gone the next week with Miss Nightingale and her staff, but that now no more nurses would be sent out until after her arrival. He took down my address and promised to write to me.

A day or two passed and then I received a letter telling me that I was not too late after all. I was fitted with a bonnet, waterproof overshoes and a cloak and then sent to be fitted with a gown. Long and short was the greatest difference between the gowns; there was not much shape in them. The clothes supplied to us were not sufficient for those who had rough and dirty work to do. Two gowns were provided and I wore them out, and three of my own besides, before I came back again. The aprons and other things were also too few, and those nurses without a stock of clothes of their own must have been in difficulties. We were allowed only one small box each by way of luggage, and were not permitted to open it until we got to Constantinople so that we had to wear the same outer clothes all the way; we were a very dirty-looking set.

We went by railway to Folkestone and crossed the Channel to Boulogne, then to Paris (where we were not fit to be seen), to Lyons, down the Rhone to Valence and thence by railway to Avignon and Marseilles, where we embarked on the *Egyptus*. Eventually we passed Scutari and arrived at Constantinople (Istanbul). We left the *Egyptus* on Monday 18th December, and travelled to Therapia (outside Istanbul, where the British Embassy had a house). Like the rest of the nurses I was very much disappointed at being sent there instead of having employment at once in some military hospital in the Crimea. I was left without knowing what I was to do, or whether I should ever be set to the work for which I had hired myself. Some of our party disgraced themselves by drunkenness, and all were discontented at being kept away from the work which they had left home and friends to do. I took my turn among the nurses who went up to the naval hospital to wash clothes for the patients. I was glad to do anything that was of use to the poor fellows.

I am sure that the committee of ladies in England did all they could to get good nurses, but they were obliged to get other people's recommendations, and could not know enough of the working classes to judge for themselves. Many women were sent out as nurses, therefore, who hd never filled any place of trust before, and were really incapable of the duties which they had undertaken. Some among them were persons of unsteady habits who, not doing well at home, hoped to fare better abroad; others were good women and excellent nurses, and deserved to be trusted.

I was one of the nurses in the last set sent for by Miss Nightingale from the group at Therapia. We arrived at the barrackroom at Scutari on Monday afternoon. We were ready for work, but nothing was given us to do. On Tuesday we had an old parcel of shirts put before us to mend, and we continued at that work until Friday afternon. I never was allowed to visit any of the wards, but I saw the patients in the long corridor through which I passed in and out. At last I was asked to go to the stores with five other nurses to sort the linen. I was shocked by its condition; if there was a pound of rotten linen there were fifty tons of it. I do not speak at random, for I am used to the weight of goods. I remarked to one of the other nurses what a sin and shame it was to see so much linen spoiled; she said that in

the main stores there was more than a hundred tons of
stores not worth a pin, and that they called them Miss
Nightingale's stores.

I never was in them, but I believe what she told me. All
those I saw had water under them and water over them,
for it thawed that day, and the melted ice and snow came
down through the roof. The linen, good and bad, had been
mixed together, and had become all rotten. It was kept in
the stable for Mr Bracebridge's little pony.

On Saturday morning I saw Mrs Bracebridge and told
her I wished to go home if I could not go to the Crimea, for
I saw I was no use where I was and had no work to do. She
promised to speak to Miss Nightingale. I had as yet never
seen Miss Nightingale.

On Monday morning at noon Miss Nightingale sent for
me and after speaking very politely and telling me to sit
down, she said, 'I understand that you have been upsetting
my nurses.'

I said, 'No, I have nothing to do with anybody but myself,
but I want to go home if I can't go to the Crimea. I don't
like this place, nor anybody in it, nor do I like the system.'

'You don't like me then?' she said.

'No, I don't,' I said, 'but I never saw you before.'

'Before you go any further,' said Miss Nightingale, 'I
want to impress on you that if you *do* go to the Crimea, you
go against my will. If you misbehave yourself there will be
no home for you here, and you will be sent straight back to
England.'

This put up my Welsh blood, and I told her that neither
man nor woman dared to accuse me of misbehaving
myself.

She informed me that she had made me over to a new
superintendant and I said (my Welsh blood being up again),
'Do you think I am a dog or an animal, to make me over to
someone else? I have a will of my own.'

I persevered in my intention of going to Balaclava, and she said, 'Well, if you do go, I have finished with you *entirely*.' In spite of this she said she would help me to get a ship there as soon as she could. Ten days later I left with a new superintendant and four other nurses for Balaclava. The voyage took two days and we then had to stay on the ship for four days before we were allowed to disembark.

We went to one of the Russian houses which was empty, adjoining the surgery. Next day the superintendant and I went to visit the wards and I shall never forget the sights I saw as long as I live. I was there from half-past eight in the morning until twelve at night. On our setting out, the superintendant told me that I was not to speak to the patients. When I got to No. 5 ward, poor fellows! 'God bless your face!' they cried out. The first man I met with, I asked how he was. The superintendant scolded me and repeated her order that I should not speak to them.

I began to open some of their wounds. The first that I touched was a case of frostbite. The toes of both feet fell off with the bandages. The hand of another man fell off at the wrist. It was between a fortnight and six weeks since the wounds of many of the men had been looked at and dressed. They had only two surgeons in attendance. One soldier there had been wounded at Alma by a shot which passed through his left breast above the heart, and came out below the shoulder-blade. His wound had not been dressed for five weeks, and I took at least a quart of maggots from it. From many of the other patients I removed them in handfuls. When the wounds were regularly attended to these men soon got well. I do not believe that maggots ever occur in cases where the wounds are properly cleaned and dressed, and always consider their presence as a proof of neglect.

Not a man there had a bed. They lay upon bunks (trestles

and boards) having one blanket under and a blanket and rug over each patient. Their greatcoats were their only pillows, and they had no sheets. The sick and the wounded were alike neglected, unclean, and covered with vermin.

That first day I only washed wounds, applied fresh poultices, and tried to relieve the discomfort of the poor creatures a little. That evening I found the deputy-purveyor and asked him about bedsteads and bedding for the hospital patients. He told me that he had plenty. I inquired whether I could have three hundred or four hundred sets by eight o'clock the next morning and he said 'Yes.' By eight the next morning he had them all put ready for me, and I immediately set the orderlies about washing and changing the clothes of the poor men. I made the beds, with blankets, sheets and pillows, all clean, and then the orderlies got the men into them. I had all this done myself, the superintendant did not interfere. She just came and looked at what was going on. That was my Saturday's work, until twelve at night.

In the weeks that followed I used to see the fatigue parties waiting to be sent to their work. Some of these men were without socks, others had worn their flannel shirts for six weeks. I often asked them if they wanted anything and told them to come to me when their day's labour was over at five o'clock. I then made a list of their wants for Mrs Shaw Stewart, and she gave me the things for each man.

She was so kind in doing this that, like a true Welsh-woman, I determined to make the most of the opportunity, and told the men in the fatigue parties to inquire who wanted anything in the camp. They soon brought down lists, signed by their officers, and Mrs Shaw Stewart gave me the clothes and other comforts to send back to their comrades; in this way two hundred shirts were sent to the 39th Regiment alone. She used to be amused at my being so busy about distributing the things and often laughed, knowing what I came for, when I knocked on her door.

In May Miss Nightingale first came to Balaclava. She continued on board ship four or five days after her arrival before she disembarked. On landing she went up at once to the camp but returned to sleep on board at night. I did not see her until the Friday after her landing. She went through the hospital on that day with Miss Wear, and came to the kitchen, where I was very busy, saying, 'How do you do, Mrs Davis?'

I answered, 'Very well, thank you' without raising my head from my work. In a minute or two I looked up and exclaimed, 'Oh! Miss Nightingale!'

'What, did you not know me?'

'Yes, Ma'am, but I should as soon have expected to see the Queen here as you.'

She afterwards went out of the kitchen. The next day I was told she had had a violent quarrel with a tipsy nurse and on the same day she was taken ill on board ship and carried up as a patient to the Castle hospital.

I do not undervalue the services of any of the ladies, but real high-born gentlewomen are not accustomed to hard manual labour, and are not strong enough for it. In performing servants' work they put constraint upon themselves and hurt the feelings of the men, who were acutely aware of the unfitness of such work for persons of high rank. Ladies may be fit to govern but for general service persons of a different class, who could put their hands to anything, were more useful.

Fragments of a Silent Life:
Elizabeth Prichard in Patagonia

Translated by EURWEN BOOTH

This material is taken from documents tucked into the front of an edition of Transactions of Welsh People in Manchester, *which is now held in the National Library of Wales at Aberystwyth (NLW MS 125 25B). The original translation from Welsh was by Eurwen Booth for Dr. Françoise Maurel of the University of Brest in Brittany, who had been directed to it by Dr. Ceridwen Lloyd-Morgan of the National Library. Together they have brought from the shadows 'a silent life'.*

Thousands of Welsh people emigrated to North America in the eighteenth and nineteenth centuries, many of them looking for a place where they could maintain their language and culture, but it became clear that English would emerge as the majority language of their new countries and that even if they managed to resist its pressure their children and grandchildren would not. In the middle of the nineteenth century Argentina welcomed immigrants from Europe who would settle in its remote southern territories, and offered a place where Welsh people could establish their own settlements free from English influence. To Michael D. Jones, the prime mover and financial supporter of a new Welsh homeland, its great advantage was that Welsh would be not only the medium of social contact and religious worship, but also of education, commerce and government. The first group of settlers sailed from Liverpool on 31 May 1865 in the ship Mimosa, *landed at Port*

Madryn on 28 July and lived for several weeks in the shelter of caves. The first years of the settlement – Y Wladfa Gymreig – were spent trying to scratch an existence out of the wild desert. As this piece shows, many settlers left and others died; their situation would have been even more desperate if the local tribe, the Tehuelche, had not taught them to hunt.

The events of Elizabeth Prichard's life can be pieced together from the bundle of documents preserved by chance because they had been put inside a volume which, also by chance, found a place in the National Library. It is significant that these events are described only from the point of view of their relevance to the lives of male members of her family and that, for example, there is no reference to her in her daughter's obituary, although the later mention of her house in relation to her son's death implies that she was still alive at the time. Betsy Cadwaladyr – assertive, independent and accustomed to making her own decisions about her life – was an exception among Welsh women travellers of her period, and the lives of most of them were far closer to Elizabeth Prichard's: unremitting hard work, physical hardship, the dangers of childbirth and illness in a remote settlement, and all the privations of life in a hostile and sometimes threatening environment. The events in her life during 1868 – her second pregnancy, the failure of her husband and the other men who had sailed with him to return, the birth of her second child, the Inquest at which her husband was declared dead, and her marriage to the man who as Registrar had married her to her first husband and as Coroner had declared him officially dead – are the stuff of melodrama, but her response to them can only be guessed at. If she had remained on her own with two small children, not only her economic but her physical survival could have been at risk in the difficult and sometimes desperate conditions of the settlement's early years; what she thought and what she felt about the direction her life had taken we can never know.

(1) A NOTE ON AN ENVELOPE ADDRESSED
     TO IONAWRYN WILLIAMS OF BETHESDA

I was married to the widow Dimol on Christmas Day
1868. The following Sunday we attended the afternoon
service, me with the boy in my arms and she with the
baby, Gwladys. At the end of the sermon the Reverend
A. Matthews baptised the girl Gwladys Dimol. In the
Seiat* afterwards I was elected Officer and Secretary of
the Chapel.

(signed) R. J. Berwyn

(2) AN OBITUARY NOTICE

DIMOL – May 13, after two days' illness, in Y Wladfa
Gymreig, aged 18 years, Gwladys, daughter of the late
T. P. E. Dimol and dear daughter of R. J. Berwyn. It has
caused a very sad feeling throughout the country
to see a young, strong, healthy girl struck down so
suddenly. A very large crowd gathered for her funeral
on 15th May, which included many young girls of the
same age. On Sunday 16th May Mr Lloyd Jones
preached on the subject in the Independents' Chapel,
as did Mr W. Roberts of Llanrwst at the Methodist
Chapel where she had been a member. At the hymn-
singing on Tusday 18th May the anthem *My days have
ended* brought very sad feelings to all when it was
sung in her memory.

---

* A meeting of the committee which organised and administered
the business of the chapel.

(3)   A NOTE ATTACHED TO ITEM 2

In the newspaper *Y Faner* I asked for information about Gwladys and her family and received the following details:

Twmi Dimol emigrated to Y Wladfa Gymreig with the first group of settlers who sailed at the end of May 1865 in the ship *Mimosa*. It was only an assumption that he and the others with him had drowned. The last seen or heard of them was that they had set sail from Del Carmen (more commonly known now as Patagones) with supplies of food and two working oxen, on their way back to Y Wladfa Gymreig. He was a relatively young man. By the beginning of 1866 his garden was the best, if not the only, garden in Y Wladfa Gymreig at the time. It was a few miles up the valley from Trerawson, near the river. (From *Yr Hen Wladfawr*/The Old Countryman, 23.6.1897)

(4)   A LETTER

Trerawson
Chubut
via Buenos Aires
December 21st 1897

Dear Mr Ionawryn Williams,

I am very happy to answer my part of the letter of September 29th 1897. I will tell you what I know of your old friend, Twmi Dimol.

Thomas Pennant Evans (Twmi Dimol) was a member of the first group of settlers who came out to Patagonia in the *Mimosa* which sailed from Liverpool at the end of May 1865. I was the Purser and he was one of the Stewards. We were very busy during the voyage, but always – before we faced the sea, while at sea, after landing – the two of us were bosom friends and there was never any sourness or bickering between us; we always saw eye to eye.

When we landed it was spring here, but our seeds did not bear fruit because it was too late in the year and the ground was too dry. Many of our company left in the first two months, and many died; from around 160, our number fell to 100.

The next year, 1866, on March 30th (his thirtieth birthday) he married Elizabeth Prichard, aged 21, who had been brought up at Tynypwll, Waenwen, Pentir, near Bangor. I have the marriage Registration Form: I was the Registrar.

This is how the wedding happened: at the time, we were building our huts on the smallholdings. We had already built the houses in the village, in a square surrounded by earthworks with four turrets and a ditch all around it which had been made by hunters twenty years previously as a defence against the Indians; we named it Caeranfur Trerawson. Around the houses we built a chapel, a storehouse, a smithy, a carpenter's shop, a cobbler's shop, a saddler's and a drapery shop, and we would meet there on Saturdays and Sundays. On Monday mornings many of us would hurry to the smallholdings to build simple huts, to prepare the ground for sowing and then to plant gardens. I worked with John Roberts and Dimol worked with the owner of the next smallholding, Rhydderch Huws of Manchester. On the last Monday in March Dimol came to me and said, 'Bring your writing materials and the Registration Book with you, because you will need them during the week.' About noon on Tuesday 30th March I heard a shout from the next hut and an orange banner was waved at me to summon me.

They had built barely a yard of wall, and there were no tables and chairs. The bride came from the town, about ten miles away, with Rhydderch Huws's wife and an old widow-woman. The meal was cooked in a clearing in the middle of the sedge; the bull-rushes had been cut down and arranged like rows of hay-sheaves.

I sat on one of these, and Rhydderch Huws held a spade level, with its handle on my knee and the Registration Book and the pens balanced on it, and the widow-woman held the ink-bottle so that it wouldn't spill, and that is how Dimol and his love pledged faithfulness till death to each other. Then we had sandwiches and tea and roast wild goose, a tasty and sustaining meal. The youngsters in the town soon heard what had happened and when the bride got back she was taken down from her horse, put into a chair and carried all round the town, with 'hurrahs!' on all sides. On Saturday night, when Dimol came to town, he got the same treatment.

Eleven months later their son Arthur Llywelyn was born; he is now a married man with children.

Dimol soon made himself famous in the area as a gardener and herbalist; he discovered thyme, rosemary, aniseed and celery among the country's native herbs, and also fennel, veronica, watercress and especially the flower that we call *Clwm Dimol* (Convolvulus Dimoli), a very pretty flower native to Patagonia.

The settlement owned a small ship (80 tons) to run from here to the Rio Negro. Only the captain was paid;

the crew was made up of men working as sailors in order to get a free passage. I and many others did this, and in 1867 Dimol started doing this work.

We know that the ship arrived at the Rio Negro and set off on the return voyage. It was carrying two working oxen and food supplies; on board were Captain Roberts Nagle of Barmouth, George Jones from Liverpool, David Davies from Aberdare, James Jones from Llanelli, Thomas Pennant Evans (Dimol) from Pennant Melangell, and Thomas Cadivor Wood, an Englishman who had learned Welsh and lived at Caerleon. The ship, the *Denby*, sailed from the Rio Negro in February 1868. Nothing more is known.

Around the end of February I and several others saw the reflection of a great fire in the sky in a southerly direction. This made us very uneasy, because we knew from experience that when Captain Nagle had taken spirits he had a habit of mistaking one cliff for another; we thought that as the cliffs on many parts of the coastline were very similar, he could easily have mistaken one inlet for another. At that time, however, communication between the small Welsh Wladfa and the rest of the great wide world was infrequent. We heard nothing to explain the light in the sky.

In May 1868 Mr Lewis Jones came with a family of immigrants and many animals to help Y Wladfa. It was a Sunday morning; the very heavy rain had washed out all the recent footprints and he was within five hundred yards of our village before he saw either man or beast. He told us that the *Denby* had sailed from the Rio Negro in February.

The wives of Dimol and James Jones were heavily pregnant, and all the men on the ship except Cadivor had relatives in the village. There was great grief and crying that afternoon: hill and valley echoed with cries of woe from mother and wife and sister and cousin for their dear ones. No more has ever been heard of the *Denby*, and no news is likely to be heard.

About two years later a whaling ship, the *Irene*, anchored near Atlas Point; its captain, Captain Wright, knew from previous voyages that there was a safe harbour there and clear water for his ship. He told us that he and his sailors went ashore to shoot ostrich or hares or whatever they could find. When they were about three miles from the sea they saw a human corpse, the body of a man, completely dried up. They lifted it up, and it crumbled away in their hands.

Other people told us later that near St. George's Channel they had seen a cross in the ground with the initials D.D. on it, and they thought that this must mark the last resting-place of David Davies from Aberdare. Some time after this Captain Wright went to Port Desire, about two hundred miles from here. When he came back he told us that in an old house, which had been deserted by refugees a hundred years ago before the War of South American Independence, he found a human body, the corpse of a man, sitting in a corner with a dish of water at its side. He described it to me, and I knew it was Captain Nagle.

Some time after this John Peters was wandering near St. George's Channel with some other men, look-ing for treasure, when they saw a man sitting under a hedge. The approached him and saw that he was dead. When they touched him, he crumbled away in their hands. From his clothes they knew it was Dimol. He was using a sail as a bed and had an extra set of clothing with him, and a watch belonging to Cadvan Gwynedd which he had been looking after. He was wearing knee breeches and a coat in the livery of the Union Club Manchester, where he had been a steward. His remains were buried where they were found; the watch and the coat buttons were given into the care of the president of the Falkland Islands, Colonel d'Arcy.

In October 1868, eight months after the *Denby* set sail, I was asked to act as Coroner in relation to the loss of the ship and the men. There were witnesses to establish that the ship had sailed from the Rio Negro; a verdict was returned that the ship had been lost somewhere along the coastline. From circumstantial evidence I deduced that the *Denby* had run aground somewhere in the Gulf of St. George, that Captain Nagle went south to Port Desire, and that the remains of at least three others show that they went north-wards.

Dimol's widow gave birth to a daughter, Gwladys, in September 1868, seven months after her husband's departure; the girl died when she was eighteen years old. When Gwladys was three months old her mother became my wife; on Christmas Day 1868 the whole of Y Wladfa Gymreig came to celebrate the wedding of Berwyn and Dimol's widow.

We had thirteen children, five sons and eight daughters. My wife's son, Arthur Llywelyn Dimol, had two sons and two daughters; one of his daughters died. He breeds animals, mainly sheep.

(signed) R. J. Berwyn

(5)   *IN MEMORIAM*

Arthur Llywelyn Dimol
25 February 1867 – 7 January 1899

died at his mother's house, Perllanhelyg, Trerawson,
Camwy Valley, Y Wladfa Gymreig, Chubut,
Patagonia, Argentina, Sud America

And the spirit returns to God, who gave it.

(6)   A NOTE INCLUDED WITH ITEM 4

It was my father who gathered together all this family
history. I don't know of anything I can add. The story
of Dimol ended twelve years before I was born. I know
nothing about it.

Wyn Berwyn

VIII

THEY GAVE US SO MUCH

The reasons for the journeys described in the two pieces in this chapter were very specific and very different from those which motivated many of the Welsh women who contributed to other chapters; whereas the others often travelled from motives of their own (for example: curiosity about another people or culture, a desire to learn more, the need for work, the wish to be with their husbands) the two writers here embarked on their trips with the aim of taking something – practical help, training, specific skills, money, encouragement, solidarity – to the people they would be staying among, who in both cases were members of a community far removed from their own geographically, culturally and linguistically. Their admiration for the communities they visited is clear, as is their gratitude for the hospitality shown to them and their respect for the courage and resilience they found in people whose daily lives were lived among so much hardship and danger; the sympathy with which they began their journeys rapidly became a deep-felt empathy.

One of the reasons for their trips was to bring support and encouragement to the communities they visited; their accounts make clear that meeting these communities had exactly the effect on the writers themselves that they were hoping to bring to the people they visited, and that by the end of their visits they felt they were privileged to have been given the chance to meet the people they had come into contact with and that they had received far more than they had given.

Many of the contributions to this book emphasise the gulf between different communities and cultures and the difficulty, if not impossibility, of real understanding between them. The pieces in this chapter suggest that while deep differences and often mutual incomprehension and mis-understanding remain, it is sometimes possible – given enough goodwill, desire to communicate and generosity of spirit on both sides – to make genuine contact, and that what the two parties have in common can, if only temporarily, be more important than what divides them.

Singing in Palestine

MARY MILLINGTON

In the spring of 1994 sixteen members of Côr Cochion Caerdydd met regularly for extra rehearsals, practised new songs, prepared special new t-shirts and generally buzzed with excitement – the usual signs of a choir about to go on tour. Some of us were a little apprehensive because this was to be no ordinary destination but a solidarity tour of occupied Palestine and parts of Israel, which had been organised under the auspices of the British Council in East Jerusalem. We would be staying in Ramallah on the West Bank.

I was one of the four altos and comparatively new to the choir, an ex-Greenham woman who had caught 'the Welsh bug' (as some people call that absolute fascination with the Welsh language which sometimes grips individuals regardless of nationality, origin or creed) from Helen Thomas, a Welsh and Welsh-speaking activist who had joined us on the Common in our protest against the nuclear missiles there. Helen, who came from Newcastle Emlyn, was tragically killed by a police horse-box at Greenham in August 1989, aged only 22. She had impressed us all with her clear politics, her warmth, her energy and goodness. I became determined to learn the beautiful language whose struggle for survival Helen had conveyed to me with such angry fervour. My search for good tuition brought me to Cardiff where I met and joined the choir; their combination of campaigning and singing in many languages (including Welsh) was irresistible to me.

The logo on our new t-shirts combined the Welsh dragon and the Palestinian flag, with the dragon making a victory sign with one claw. We had learned two songs in Arabic, *Yamma mwail illhawa* (Lament of a Mother) and *Mowtini* (My Homeland). All that remained was for us to do our best to communicate with the Palestinian people, learn more about them, and make some contribution towards their struggle against injustice.

We arrived in Tel Aviv on 19th April 1994 in a tense atmosphere following the Hebron massacre (the massacre at the mosque in Hebron of 29 Palestinians by Israeli settlers). We were driven straight to our billet in Ramallah, the Evangelical school for Boys and Girls run by the Reverend Audi Rantisi, a greatly-respected peace activist who in 1949 had been force-marched from his village near Tel Aviv along with whole communities of Palestinians, never to see it again. He and his wife managed to provide us with a secure base at a time when food and resources were scarce for everybody in the Occupied Territories. Sometimes we would hear gunfire or smell burning tyres from the comparative safety of the residential block. Above all, our hosts were prepared to answer our questions and give us background information. We realised that we were very privileged to be there.

As a woman and a feminist I was especially eager to listen to Palestinian women, and I was not disappointed. On our first day we visited the Society of In'ash el-Usra in El-Bireh, which is a woman-led charity providing nursery education and also paid employment for the widows of the *intifada*, as well as education and training. The Deputy President spoke eloquently to us, giving us the clear historical background and overview that we needed. We sang to the nursery-school children, and watched entranced as they performed an action song about the olive tree, symbol of the Palestinian struggle. These tiny children had no choice but to become politically aware: they needed to know why their fathers had died. We were given a translation of the words they were singing, which were full of aspirations for peace and hope for the future. I cannot help wondering, as I write this now, how many of those children are still alive and, of those that are, how much hope they have in their hearts in the face of continued illegal occupation, escalating injustices and violence.

Our visit to Gaza gave another great experience of woman-power. We dropped into the Y.M.C.A. to see some children's art. In particular I remember a series of drawings by a fifteen-year-old girl recording events in the *intifada* that she had witnessed: young boys with bags over their heads being beaten by Israeli soldiers, and other horrors. Then our host said that a women's meeting was in progress; the International Women's Day celebrations on March 8th had been postponed because of the Hebron massacre, and the women were planning an event in May. Our host asked them if they would like Côr Cochion Caerdydd to sing to them during their lunch break, and to our joy they said Yes.

The previous day we had been impressed by a highly-educated middle-class Palestinian woman who communicated eloquently with us in English; now we were faced with a hall full of working-class Palestinian women of all ages with their babies, all with covered heads and in long dresses, the older ones in hand-embroidered traditional costume. They had no word of English and we had no word of Arabic, but they began to communicate with us immediately. They tittered a little as we sang our songs in Arabic (we were told afterwards that some of our mis-pronunciations changed the meaning of the words in a very unfortunate way), but when we sang *Women of the Working Class*, the anthem of the Miners' Strike, and someone translated it for them, they rose as one woman, smiling and making victory signs above their heads. As we sang 'We are women, we are strong' some of them surged on to the stage to join us; their energy was almost a tangible force. After singing we ate with them, they asked to be photographed with us, they handed over their lovely babies for us to talk to in universal baby-language, and we had no communication difficulties at all.

We were told that these families had no money; their menfolk had been accustomed to going over into Israel to work, but the border had been closed to them after the Hebron massacre and so they had no wages. The women survived by sharing, borrowing and helping each other. We were filled with admiration for their strength and spirit.

We met the same spirit in the refugee camps, in particular Jabaliya camp in Gaza and Deheisha camp near Bethlehem. We were overwhelmed by the generosity and hospitality of people living on next to nothing, with Israeli soldiers looking down into their homes from watch-towers. They had access to water for only one hour a day, while nearby Israeli settlements had as much water as they wanted to run washing-machines and clean cars, yet the women in the camps managed to keep their houses and their families' clothes spotlessly clean in squalid conditions without functioning sewerage systems. Somehow, in spite of all this, again and again families would manage to take the sixteen of us into their homes and provide cool lemonade and cakes.

Now, as I stand on draughty pavements protesting at the increasing attacks by a rich state which is armed to the teeth on these desperately poor people whose land is being systematically stolen from them, I feel that I can never repay that unquestioning friendliness and hospitality. I feel ashamed that although I have been active in the Palestinian Solidarity Campaign, although we have raised money and written letters, the plight of our Palestinian friends goes on getting worse and worse.

During our fortnight in Palestine and Israel we had the opportunity to meet many different people and do many things; we met cultural and artistic groups, we were taken on sight-seeing tours, we went to parties and picnics. As well as Palestinians we met Israelis, both Arab and Jewish, who were active for peace and justice, people who had the courage to criticise their government and provide legal representation and moral support for Palestinians. As I write, I know they are organising peace rallies at Israeli border check-points.

But the memories that come back most often and most strongly are of ordinary women surviving, laughing, protesting, and generously welcoming the stranger with the pain of losing husbands and children still fresh in their hearts.

A Month in Eritrea

ELIZABETH HARRIS

Thumping rhythms invade my sleep: it's Saturday night in Surbiton, and the hotel disco is at its peak. Full of excitement and lying in an unfamiliar bed I realise that this time tomorrow I will be 3,000 miles away in the Horn of Africa, in the small country of Eritrea. Louise, my room-mate, stirs. I have known her for only twenty-four hours, but will spend the next month in her company. We seem to get on well despite the age-gap: she is 21, the same age as my daughter, and similar in age to the three other girls in our seven-strong team. Selected from the four countries of Britain, we are all volunteers on a Tearfund charity project to work in a Christian school and orphanage. As the disco winds down I collect my thoughts. Our day of 'cultural orientation' has offered plenty of advice to concentrate the mind: attempt to learn the language, don't go out alone, use your right hand for eating, boil water for drinking, drink frequently, use mosquito nets, dress modestly keep-ing arms and legs covered, and above all be prepared to adapt to whatever presents itself. My mind is still buzzing as I slide into sleep, dreaming of giant mosquitoes.

By Day Three we are installed in a simple bungalow, complete with flush toilet and bath but limited water. The journey here was a kaleidoscope of impressions: towards the end of a tedious seven-hour flight my window seat afforded me a glimpse of the lunar-like landscape of North

Africa. On arriving at Asmara's no-frills airport, we were greeted warmly by a young man named Abraham; bulging rucksacks were loaded onto the roof-rack of an ancient minibus, together with several sacks of meal and a live goat. We set off on the hour-long drive to Decamhare, bumping through biblical scenery featuring laden donkeys, a camel train, giant cacti, roadside fruit-sellers and, at every turn, children laughing, shouting and pointing at our white faces through a haze of dust and exhaust fumes.

*   *   *

I'm recovering beneath my mosquito net from a bone-shaking 170 km. round trip to Adi Quala school. Most of the journey, in a battered landcruiser, was over rough earth, stone tracks, and dry riverbeds. Our tour of the school has made a deep impression on us. Each dingy classroom was packed with up to sixty very basic desks; there were no books, nothing on the walls, no paper or resources of any kind. The headmaster explained that each teacher has one copy of the textbook, and the children are expected to provide their own pencils and paper. None of the teachers has had any formal training; they teach two shifts a day in order to give as many children as possible the chance of a little education. We were given lunch by the headmaster's wife in their little two-roomed house. The staple food of Eritrea was served in a huge communal dish: *injera* looks a bit like an enormous pancake, but is an unappetising greyish colour with a damp bubbly texture. It has a sour, fermented taste and was served without any accompaniments which would have helped us get it down. I surprised myself by adjusting to it quite quickly, while some of the team were doing more heaving than swallowing. Strong sweet black tea was also served, and this we drank with relish. Next we were introduced to the delights of the 'long drop' toilet, where my somewhat rusty squatting skills were put to the test and found wanting. Rattling back to the relative luxury of the bungalow in Decamhare I began to wonder how on earth we would fulfil our obligation to help train teachers whose circumstances and resources are so far removed from ours.

After three days of teachers' training we are still struggling to pitch our sessions appropriately, and our students are having difficulty in following our distinctive accents: Welsh, Irish and Scots! Today we led a session on mixed ability groups, although we all doubted its relevance where classes of up to sixty are the norm and books are a rare luxury. Apparently if a pupil fails to make the grade he is simply kept back for a year, and if he fails again he has to leave. Pastor Okba urged us to continue despite our misgivings: 'We must learn about your methods if we are to catch up in the world. It may not seem relevant to the teachers now, but it will become so as our situation changes.'

The children's games sessions are a great success, especially when we use our colourful 'parachute', which produces whoops of delight each time it's pulled out of its bag. Most of the children are barefoot, but during the football sessions some of the boys share a pair of plastic sandals so that they can protect their 'kicking' foot. One little girl about seven years old participated fully in every activity with her baby brother strapped to her back. I was so moved by this that I offered to hold him for a while. She looked unsure but wanted to oblige me and duly untied her brother. The baby looked at me, began to wail pitifully, and continued to do so until he was safely reunited with his sister.

*   *   *

We are invited to coffee at the home of one of the orphan-age mothers. Unaware of the ceremony involved, I envisage an hour of Cardiff-style chatting over mugs of instant coffee. Everyone is invited to sit with the hostess who takes a handful of green coffee beans, drops them into a shallow pan and roasts them over a small charcoal fire. Next she grinds them with a pestle and mortar and tips them into a black clay coffee-pot which is filled with water and placed in the fire. Meanwhile maize kernels are tossed in a large lidded pan over the fire, to make popcorn. While she is working, Teras talks to us, asking about our work and our families. Her English-language skills are limited, but her hospitality is wonderful. She encourages us to take large handfuls of salted popcorn while she pours the coffee, stuffing the spout with a tuft of curly hair to act as a filter. The tiny cups have been primed with sugar and she hands them round; the coffee is syrupy black and hot. Politeness requires us to drink a minimum of three cups each, with plenty more on offer. Between servings we are exhorted to sing, and our shared background of evangelical Christianity makes this surprisingly easy. The words of familiar hymns and worship songs take on a new and moving significance as we sit in the tiny house of this gracious woman, whose possessions are few but whose generosity towards us seems boundless. I struggle to express my appreciation as we say goodbye and go out squinting into the bright sunshine, where chickens scratch and peck. Life seems to have slowed right down, and deepened somehow.

*   *   *

One afternoon our new young friend Moses and some of the other teenage boys take us walking in the hills. They catch small frogs and crickets, and collect porcupine spines to give us. About halfway up the hill we pass the town burial-ground, where sheep and goats graze among the gravestones. When we stand on the rocky summit it is like going back in time. With no traffic noise I can hear the sound of the children's voices as they play in the street below, and the occasional braying of a donkey. It seems so peaceful here, though yesterday we visited another hillside and saw the rotting boots and bleached bones of soldiers left where they fell during the war with Ethiopia. As we go back down the hill Moses and the others tell us the names of the different kinds of rocks – basalt, granite and sandstone – and talk about their president who, like them, has a biblical name (Isaac) and is only forty-two. They tell us that he and the president of Ethiopia went to the same school, which is one reason why they have managed to negotiate peace between their two countries.

As we get back to the orphanage compound a young man meets us and breaks the news that one of the evangelists has just died; she was six months pregnant and collapsed earlier today. There is an almost tangible sense of grief here in the compound: everyone is silent and subdued. On our way to the bungalow we hear distant wailing, but no one is around and doors are closed. Later that evening I walk round the compound. According to their custom the adults of the community are gathered outside the house where the woman died. They sit on benches, heads covered, singing and crying. Some of the women are sifting through large round trays of lentils. A small fire burns on the ground. Some of us sit with them. One of the pastors gives a short sermon, others pray. The vigil continues all night.

In the morning Pastor Okba explains that all work is suspended and that we will be taken to the funeral in Asmara. The rest of the community is piling into a battered bus as we set off in the relative comfort of the minibus, driven by Abraham. Later, outside a small house in the city, a rough wooden coffin is loaded on to the back of an open van. Women are wailing and clinging to each other. I am swept along in the huge crowd that forms the funeral procession. A miasma of smells curls up through the mid-day heat, making my head reel. Despite the team's efforts to stay together we are soon scattered among the crowd, and I begin to fear the potential dangers. We were ill-prepared for this situation and Peter, the electrician who has been working long hours to complete the school's wiring, is not carrying his water bottle.

For nearly two hours the procession weaves its tortuous way across the city centre until we reach the burial ground, where a service is held and the coffin is lowered into a concrete-lined pit and sealed with flagstones. There is a flurry of activity as the crowd disperses, and I discover that Louise has fainted at the roadside. We give her water, and someone provides an umbrella for shade. We are taken to a restaurant, where we rest for a couple of hours. That even-ing we are all in various states of exhaustion and no one can eat the *cawl* I have prepared as therapy.

The next morning reveals Peter to be frighteningly ill. He has become totally dehydrated due to sickness and diar-rhoea, and is unable to keep down even a sip of water. We put him in my bed because it is nearest the bathroom and continue to ply him with dehydration fluid. Tomorrow is to be our weekend break, scuba-diving in the Red Sea. After a couple of hours, much prayer and no improvement we decide to ask Pastor Okba if there is any possibility of finding a doctor; after all, we can afford to pay. I am think-ing of how different it was for the dead young woman and her unborn child when Peter suddenly staggers out of bed and collapses on the concrete floor. I kneel beside him, searching for vital signs. At the same moment a man enters the bungalow.

'Are you the doctor?' asks Louise.

She's delirious, I think despairingly.

'Yes,' says the young man, and immediately comes to Peter and assesses the situation. We carry him back to bed and the doctor rigs up a bottle of plasma, which is the only intravenous fluid that we have in our emergency medical kit.

'It's too thick, really, but better than nothing,' he observes and then leaves quickly, saying he will be back with some saline solution. We wait in silent agony. Peter is completely unconscious. Doctor Berhane returns after about an hour, but without the saline drip.

'I'll have to go to Asmara to get it,' he says, checking Peter's pulse and blood pressure. 'You'll have to get some more fluid into him.' He shows me how to lift Peter's head and dribble the tiniest drops into his mouth. 'Do it every ten minutes, even if he complains.'

Over the next two hours Peter writhes with stomach cramps every time I give him water. I keep thinking he is going to choke and I bend close to him as his lips move, wondering in horror whether I am listening to the last words of a dying man.

At last the doctor returns and rigs up the drip, instructing me how to change to the second bag of saline solution and remove it when all the fluid has gone through. He is anxious to leave before dark; in Eritrea it's unwise to drive alone at night. The next day Peter is pale but conscious and we are already cheering up, even though the Red Sea trip is off.

*   *   *

We have just returned from an overnight visit to Senafe. A young man called Kifili sat in the back of the minibus with us. Hermone, a pastor's wife and unusually large for an Eritrean, took up two seats in the front. They were both going to visit relatives. The terrain was breathtakingly mountainous, with scores of hairpin bends and switch-backs. Kifili soon lost the contents of his stomach and I only managed to hang on to mine by jamming my legs down the side of the seat so that I could face forwards and stare out front. At one point we were looking *down* onto mountain tops capped with little clouds. We passed the time by singing every song we could think of, and Kifili taught us an Eritrean worship song.

Senafe was staging a torrential thunderstorm when we arrived and checked into a hotel which had Italian food and clean rooms. The electric lighting was intermittent but candles were provided, and we spent the night in comfort. Early on Sunday morning we went sightseeing: a 2,500-year-old Axumite settlement of complex buildings, impressive stone staircases and interconnecting underground passages. A bearded old man showed us round. At first he prevaricated: where was our official pass? The offer of 25 birr seemed to solve the problem, even to the extent of allowing us to photograph him. En route to church we passed a dead donkey lying in the middle of the road, bloated and flyblown. We packed into a tiny building and were invited to bring greetings and songs. Compared to our ragged rendering the church choir of four sang superbly, and the sermon lasted a mere hour and ten minutes (all in Tigrinya, of course). During the proceedings village children shouted and threw stones at the building.

The drive back to Decamhare was even more hair-raising than the outward journey because we went even faster and Hermone was sick. This did not prevent her from insisting that we stop to buy a whole sack of cactus fruit from a roadside stall, nor from proceeding to eat them as if she was under contract to finish the lot before we got back. Perhaps they have anti-travelsickness properties, because she was fine for the rest of the journey.

Our last day was spent as guests at Moses's sister's wedding. At the church service early in the morning the bride and groom knelt facing the congregation to make their vows and sign a register. They were each given a small candle to light a larger one, which they both held. The church was decorated with streamers of pink toilet-tissue and the choir, dressed in long green robes, made a truly joyful noise. Before he began his eighty-minute sermon, the preacher asked nursing mothers to start breastfeeding their babies in order to keep them quiet. Afterwards came the eight-hour reception; under makeshift canopies bottles of soft drinks were set out, and mountains of *injera* were served with rich spicy sauces. Women squatted on the ground to wash the dishes, while children played and posed in their finery. The best man introduced himself to us as 'the first man of the broom'. After the meal the bride and groom led us on a walking tour which would have left a sherpa breathless. The choir still sang, and photos were taken before we went to a new venue for yet more refreshments. We felt wholeheartedly included in the joyful atmosphere, though for us it was tinged with sadness at our imminent departure. Early evening saw our reduced belongings piled with us into the minibus, and we waved goodbye. My last glimpse of the now familiar faces was obscured in a haze of dust and tears.

*   *   *

Somewhere in the sky over Europe, feeling in dire need of a bath and lashings of moisturiser. My painful sadness at leaving has subsided into wistful regret that my adventure has come to an end. The trip has taught me a lot about how much I take for granted, how little I know about other cultures, how real faith works, and how important human relationships are. I think I am not quite the same person as when I left home a month ago: I went to teach and to give, but I feel that I am the one who has learned and received much more from the generosity of others.

IX

WHERE DO I BELONG?

It is often the people of a smaller country, or one which feels itself under threat, who spend much time considering what sort of people they are and where their uniqueness lies; the people of a more powerful and successful country tend to take its power and status for granted and to feel that they know exactly who they are (i.e. better than everyone else). The experience of travelling can open up these issues by putting travellers in situations which lead them to question the assumptions they have learned from the communities they live in, and by making them aware of the extent to which their own ideas and attitudes have been shaped by them. Many of the contributors to this collection have been circling round questions of personal and national identity, how they are constructed, and the way they relate to each other; the two pieces in this chapter deal with them directly.

They are written by women whose personal and national identities relate to Wales and also to another country. One comes from an Italian family in Swansea, the other from a Jewish family in Cardiff; both have strong roots in their parts of Wales and great affection for the cities they grew up in, and at the same time feel strong ties to the countries from which they derive their ancestry and religion. Their first visits to Italy and Israel respectively impelled them to analyse both their relationship with the country they visited and with Wales on their return; each had to consider, more directly and explicitly than most of us, exactly where 'home' is. If Italy is the ancestral and cultural homeland of one and Israel the religious homeland of the other, what is their relation to Wales, where they were born and grew up and where they and their families live?

It is impossible to write or say two words at exactly the same time and therefore impossible to give them exactly the same status; one has to come first and the other second, and the order which is chosen reveals which is the more important element. Both writers here offer two descriptions of themselves with the same elements in a different order, as if it was impossible for them to choose which was the more important; one begins by referring to herself as 'Latin-Celtic' and then reverses this to 'Welsh-Italian', while the other makes her difficulty clear by describing herself as 'a Jewish Welsh woman or a Welsh Jew'. The first writes 'I cross two cultures in my life on this earth' and the second describes herself as feeling 'torn' between her two countries and as having to 'balance' her love for them both. Balancing two competing allegiances is rarely easy or comfortable, but travelling from one country to another, very different, one and knowing that they are both home – if in different senses – can certainly concentrate the mind powerfully on exactly what the words 'home' and 'abroad' mean.

Schoolbooks in Spaghetti Paper

PAULETTE PELOSI

It was my first teenage year – 1967. At this famously sensitive age I suffered an upsetting transition; I'd gone to bed the night before as a young Latin-Celtic beauty (or so I seemed to Papa's camera lens) with long chestnut hair and big brown eyes, and the following morning I emerged from the opticians with a monster attached to my face: 1960s spectacle frames.

To myself at least, I had suddenly become 'plain ugly'. I needed a diversion – I went abroad, to 'the Continent', 'overseas'. My parents paid the enormous sum of 43 guineas for my school trip to Interlaken. I was lucky; some pupils had parents who worked hard to get the cash together somehow while others, whose parents worked just as hard, had to settle for summer at home in Swansea.

I think a major decider for me was the mountains. My father had talked and talked of how I would be impressed by the magical mountains – how often he had, almost breathlessly as though at altitude, described how beautiful the scenery would be and how much affected he knew I would be. In his mind's eye he was travelling through the mountains of his ancestors in the Comino Valley of central Italy, but the chance had come for me to see the mountains of Switzerland – so of course I was going. I had been taken by the nuns at my convent-school to see the film of *The Sound of Music*, so I thought I knew all about mountains.

Switzerland, Austria, Italy . . . all the same, weren't they? Weren't they?

I enjoyed my first trip abroad and came home to write in my Letts Schoolgirl's Diary 'I love Switzerland'. And I *did* love those mountains. I remember the exact moment an especially large one appeared in front of our coach, like some friendly ghost magically gathering every ray of available pure white light and projecting it en masse into our coach – breathtaking! – (can you hear a 'but' about to arrive?) but something was wrong, missing, incomplete. I found it impossible to 'connect'. I felt emotionally stranded on my own island of confusion. What did it matter – it was to be taken and enjoyed just as a precious holiday, wasn't it? In retrospect I can recall that everything from the alpine horn souvenir to the menu of horsemeat and French fries cooked in some nameless oil or fat (that I felt disinclined to smell) didn't really do much for me. After all, I wasn't Swiss, was I? I was Italian – Welsh-Italian, to boot!

Everyone at school recognised that I was Italian – was 'different'. I had a funny surname, which although it seemed relatively short and easy to pronounce as 'foreign' names go seemed to be mainly mispronounced by others. In convent-school I was the girl whose exercise books were instantly recogniseable because they were covered in the famous deep-blue paper used to package spaghetti. My mother was Anglo-Welsh but she loved to eat pasta and garlic along-side the regular egg and chips she served up to customers in our café.

Food was always a top priority for us all. I loved the indescribably gorgeous aromas of roasted peppers, pasta, sauces and soups which would fill the air in my Nonna Carmela's house in Swansea. The delicious smells would burst out into the street when the front door was opened to admit Papa and me after Sunday Mass. I was a real Welsh-

Italian Bisto Kid, my nostrils dilated to inhale all the marvellous smells and aromas of my Italian grandmother's culinary delights.

For as long as I could recall, my father had told a million vivid stories about his lovingly-remembered boyhood – a childhood spent in Italy. In recent years he remarked that I had had the 'grace' to listen and retain what he had said. But why wouldn't I? Who could refuse to be interested in his incredibly-detailed visual and aromatic memories? I could easily visualise my grandparents' village of Vallegrande in the province of Picinisco, could time-travel to their villa of Collemorelle with its olive and fig trees and its well of cold clear water, and hear the excitement of my father and his brothers and sisters when their Mamma came home from the market in Atina with wonderfully exciting purchases in her basket.

The stress of running the café all day long had taken its toll on my family: my parents parted company when I was fourteen. When I was a child we didn't have holidays: we would spend Thursday afternoons (when the café was closed) at a picnic in a local park, and that was it. We were enslaved by the café. Anyway, everyone advised my father not to return to Italy for surely, they said, everything would have changed. And I suffered years of ill-health which was finally diagnosed as Lupus, an auto-immune disorder. But at last, in 1992, I had an opportunity to accompany my father on his first return visit in sixty years to his beloved Italy.

As my father and I went through Arrivals at Fiumicino Airport in Rome, the crowds of Italians waiting at the barriers for their returning families seemed to hold eye-contact immediately . . . brown eyes to brown eyes. I felt we were at home together.

This feeling got stronger throughout the holiday. Up in

the beautiful Comino Valley of Lazio I remembered the words said in Wales: 'It will all have changed'. Things had mostly remained fundamentally the same, thank God – the same as my father had described them. We shopped for delicious fresh produce at the Monday market at Atina just as my grandmother had done. The family home of Collemorelle was still standing; the thick walls, the balcony and the *cantina* sent out hospitable ghosts to greet us. As I looked out from the balcony I was sure I glimpsed my father, the boy Mario Luigi, pulling out a mattress to spend a night under the stars; as I looked into a downstairs room I'm sure I saw them all gathered round the fire of oak logs, *pignata* of water coming to the boil, the words of the rosary in all the voices together, the young and not so young.

A million little things marched with our own ways of doing things. Everything connected with food was a religion in itself, and quality, quantity, temperature and presentation were of prime importance – the culinary commandments were obeyed on every occasion. Food was not to be played with and did not have to be moulded into cartoon shapes and colours to entice children to eat. Children ate the same food as adults from an early age. People held eye-contact, were constantly and effortlessly tactile, reacting visibly to joy and sadness. Young people had no problem respecting the old and genuinely seemed to choose and enjoy the company and wisdom of their elders. We seemed to know how we were being received, and not have to go over the events of each day anxiously in our heads and wonder if we had done the right thing and if people liked us.

Holiday's end: we returned to Wales. We felt the rain in our fingers and toes, even though it was August. Pa insisted on wearing his jacket. Even the rain seemed cruelly different: in Italy Pa had pointed out that 'the rain came down, apologised and went away'. He wrote in his diary:

'I'm back now, coping with mild holiday hangover. It's not going too well. It's almost a week since I got back and I feel I need decompressioning, like a diver.' This happened increasingly each time we came back from our successive visits to Italy. Each time we returned to our lovely friendly Wales Pa and I just felt more and more unsettled, and seemed to notice the differences more and more.

The fundamentals of living in a Catholic country go through every aspect of life and culture like wording through a stick of rock, but the way I was brought up within Catholicism in Wales was very different from being a Catholic in Italy. A feast-day in Italy is an opportunity to have fun, but the religious theme of the celebration is expected and enjoyed by both locals and tourists. A Bank Holiday in the U.K. is completely different. Sadly, it is common to read or hear later that the day was not a success because of bad weather or traffic jams. The comforting reliability of celebrations focusing on a beloved saint are missing.

The drinking of wine (and water) with meals in our part of Italy is relaxing for drinkers and those with them who may choose to have just a coffee; both want to share tthe same friendly space. In Italy I am totally relaxed in the many café-bars where all generations meet and mingle safely. An extension of this socialising is the nightly *passagiata*, a leisurely stroll through the town or village with people of all ages happily ending the day together. In Wales the attitude to alcohol is much more problematic, and these days I'm increasingly fearful of the bad behaviour of people who have drunk too much; I regularly hear others (women, especially) saying that they're too afraid to go out in the evenings, and I cannot imagine a *passagiata* in the city where I live. This saddens me deeply.

Of all the contrasts I notice between Wales and Italy, the

greatest is in attitudes to food. In Italy food is everything and one can always find freshly-cooked 'natural' meals. In parts of Wales where fast-food outlets and pubs serve processed 'instant' meals, standards are low. This is especially true perhaps for vegetarian meals. These standards are getting lower and the prices are getting higher. People grumble about this, but no one does anything.

There are also big differences on an emotional level. I'm a spontaneous person who shows my feelings, and in Italy that's no problem. Here I often have to modify my reactions to avoid being misinterpreted; I have to stop and think before I touch.

This year I lost my strongest personal link with Italy when my dear father died. I have lost a special relationship which is rare between parent and child, and my mourning has no limit of time.

I cross two cultures in my life on this earth. My father and I shared a weakness for gadgets, one of which was a daft dipping duck made of a thick plastic tube which could contain fluid; it would gradually fill up with each dip into water, finally dropping the duck's head down into the water and causing the duck to rise again to repeat the process. Like that daft duck, I continue to dip my beak into the water (and mountains) of Italy only to swing back to my pedestal base, Wales. This seemingly perpetual motion only works if each part of the equation stays the same: remove the water from the dipping duck, or the duck from the water, and he stops. One day part of my own equation may change or be removed, and I will stop.

Will I stay in Wales or Italy? Only time will decide.

Homelands

STELLA LEVEY

1956 – the year of the Suez crisis. I travelled overland to Marseilles and sailed to Israel on the oldest boat of the Zim Line. The *Negbah* had been an immigrant ship and it was very basic indeed. My accommodation was down in the hold, next to the engine room, and the heat and noise eventually drove me to sleep on the deck at night. The sea was rough, and the moon and stars kept revolving round the mast.

Five days later it was 'Land Ahoy!' and everyone rushed up on deck. There in the bright morning sunshine the Holy Land lay glittering on the horizon like a tiara. As we approached Israel, the golden glow of the dome of the Baha'i temple on Mount Carmel signalled my imminent arrival at the port of Haifa. There to meet me was my married sister, Marilyn Corne, and her friend Leila Seager, who were already living in Israel. They said I was hard to recognise: above a deeply-tanned face my highlighted strip of hair had bleached white in the sun.

Israel: land of the dream of countless Jews over centuries. I could not believe I had arrived, and I knelt down to kiss the ground at the quayside. After all the formalities were over, and after experiencing the unaccustomed heat and clamour of the day and the excitability of the Israelis and Arabs, I was carted off by open lorry up Mount Carmel, heading north for Kibbutz Rosh HaNikrah on the Lebanese border. Darkness fell early but the day's heat still lingered in the air. I marvelled at the people sitting on their balconies chattering away, at them strolling in the streets at such a late hour, at the heady smell of the trees and shrubs and flowers; I was transported to another world with a feeling of elation I had never previously experienced. I had been abroad before, but that had been in Europe. Here I was in the Middle East in a country that had been Palestine, a stamp in my album and always the impossible dream.

I spent my first night in Israel on a camp bed in a tent – no sleeping bags on the floor as in *Habonim*, the youth camps back home. There were scorpions around and I was warned not to leave my shoes on the ground in case one decided to spend the night there and then stung my foot in the morning. That was something I had never had to worry about before.

However, I had no time to dwell on such things. There were bananas to look after. I had to rise at 4 a.m., shower and dress, grab a drink and jump on the lorry bound for the banana plantation. Work was hot and tiring, and that was why there was an early start. The sun at 5 a.m. burnt through my cotton headgear as, armed with a machete, I stripped the leaves from the banana plants so that the radiant heat could reach the bunches of bananas to ripen them. This was work as I had never experienced it before and, desperate for a drink, I would throw myself prone on the muddy ground and gulp water from the holes in the irrigation pipe. I couldn't wait for 9 o'clock to come so that I could go back for breakfast – I felt I had done a day's labour in those few but very long hours. What an initiation into the adult world and the work ethic.

I'm Cardiff-born and Cardiff-bred, and proud of it. As a child I had holidayed with my parents and sister once very briefly in West Wales and for a fortnight in North Wales, both post-war holidays. In 1946 the journey to Tenby took four hours each way in a small black Standard Eight; this turned out to be a one-night stay owing to my parents' objection to American soldiers walking through our bed-room in order to gain access to theirs. The scenery, however, was impressive, for I had never been out of Cardiff before except when we would drive to a Radyr farm to avoid the bombing. In 1948 we trundled off again, bound for Llan-dudno via the Horseshoe Pass on a terrifying narrow road around the mountains where it was almost impossible to pass another vehicle. The views rivalled any photographs I had seen of alpine scenery, and the potential drop over the edge was enough to take your breath away. Beads of sweat broke out on my father's forehead, and Mam glared at Marilyn and me to stop arguing 'as Daddy has to con-centrate on his driving'. This was when I embarked on a love-affair with Wales.

This lovely country, whose citizens traditionally regarded themselves as one of the Lost Tribes, compared in size to Israel; indeed, you could travel the length of it from north to south in the same time. Why, even the churches and chapels had biblical names which we marvelled at on the occasional Sunday drives through the Valleys with my parents. This was when I started to relate Wales to the land of Israel in my mind; its biblical tone seemed more Jewish than any other place I had visited.

Wales had welcomed both sets of my grandparents – and many other members of their families escaping from the pogroms of Eastern Europe – into the Welsh Valleys, and gave them a chance to earn an honest penny. My mother's father, Gabriel Danovitch, struggled up and down moun-tains with a pack on his back, selling gas mantles for house lighting. He spoke only a little English – 'Will you buy?' – but was greeted warmly and offered mugs of hot tea

wherever he went. He later set up shop in Mary Ann Street
and then in Bridge Street in central Cardiff. My father,
Sidney Schiller (known as Mr Sinclair) and my uncles
Joseph and Maurice Danovitch (known as Mr Jordan and
Mr Dennis) followed in turn, trudging through the Valleys,
toting heavy suitcases of goods. In wartime many Jews
changed their Polish/German-sounding names to anglicised
ones to avoid anti-semitic jibes.

The State of Israel, after independence in 1848, opened its
doors to Jews of all nationalities, of all colours and of any
or no level of religious observance; it became the homeland
for survivors of the Holocaust, people who had been
driven out of their lands by Hitler and who had lost every
member of their families. But whereas crossing from Wales
to England was merely passing a sign that said 'Welcome
to England' on one side and 'Croeso i Gymru' on the other,
travelling in Israel meant you were always close to its
borders with its neighbouring enemies – Egypt, Lebanon
and Jordan – and journeys were fraught with danger. On
the train from Jerusalem to Tel Aviv there was always a
soldier in my carriage with a gun on a tripod aiming out of
the open window as the train passed a mere couple of
yards from the border.

The language did not bother me. I learned to read and
write Hebrew as a child for the purpose of praying in syna-
gogue. The only thing that was different was the accent; at
home we prayed in an Askenazi accent (that of European
Jews) and in biblical Hebrew, but in Israel it was a Sephardi
accent, similar to that of Spanish and Portuguese Jews but
with a stronger, more gutteral accent – the language of
Eliezer Ben Yehuda, the father of modern Hebrew. But
I was young and it was no effort to pick up this 'new'
language; I could make myself understood in *Ivrit* with
little difficulty.

I learned to travel around Israel on my own, jumping on and off buses which, in the countryside, carried squawking chickens as well as me and my fellow-passengers. I hitched lifts and caught trains (an experience in itself, with hordes of people all trying to do the same thing with much pushing and shoving). Nothing was on time. Queues didn't exist but if I tried to 'jump' what I thought was a queue I was soon volubly reminded of my place in it. If I asked for directions the answer was always *l'ma'alah* (a bit further on), accompanied by a casual wave of the hand. Pavements were non-existent in some places and I had to walk in the road, except that it was usually a sandy or rocky path with potholes. I spent a lot of money stopping frequently at stalls selling *mitz tapuz* (orange juice), and it was as fresh and delicious as it could be since each stall had an orange-squeezing machine and the oranges had ripened in the warmth of the sun, not in a ship's hold.

A white ball of heat blazed down relentlessly. Mornings began at the unholy hour of 4 a.m. with a bright blue clear sky. Night fell early and swiftly with very little twilight, yet life hummed in the streets. People visited each other, or sat on balconies with cold drinks at their elbows or at pavement tables outside cafés. Cooling fans revolved furiously as Israelis vigorously debated, equally noisily, Life and Politics: the issues of the day and whether David Ben Gurion, the first Prime Minister, was doing a good job. It seems that in politics there are as many opinions as there are Israelis.

For the first time in my life I felt proud to be a Jew. Everyone around me was a Jew. I was not used to this. The dustman, shop assistant, cook, waiter and toilet cleaner, who all had their own views to air vociferously, had come from many different countries after the State of Israel was established in 1948, a mere eight years previously. I was often served by people with numbers tattooed on their arms: survivors of the Holocaust, who had experienced the inhumanity of man to man as never before in history. When I visited Jerusalem and *Migdal David* (the Tower of David) I felt sickened by an exhibition of lampshades made by the Nazis out of human skin, and the bars of soap made from the fat of their victims. Suddenly all I had read in the book my mother had given me as a child, *The History of World War Two*, with its chapters on Nazi atrocities, on the concentration camps and mass graves, meant something real to me and I grew up overnight. I was a Jew, I was a woman, I was alive even though members of my family had perished in Auschwitz. I was lucky to live in Wales.

I returned to what I, Jewish Welshwoman or a Welsh Jew, considered my secular homeland, the country of my birth (and I am always proud to say I live in Wales, not in Great Britain). I marvelled at its lush foliage. It was a world away from the heat and sand, the parched deserts slowly becoming alive and blooming in the burning sun of Israel, Land of the Bible and of my Jewish religion.

I have visited Israel often since then. The difference is that now I arrive by plane, not by boat. The exotic scents in the warm air are just as vivid as I remember from my first visit, but my arrival is not heightened now by the anticipation of seeing the golden land shimmering on the horizon. Conversely, on my return to Wales I am always thrilled to see the cloudy skies and feel the blessed rain that Israel prays for instead of the blazing sun in a bright blue heaven, and to catch sight of the sign *Caerdydd* which to me means 'home': home where I was lucky to be born and to live.

Yet I am always eager to visit Israel again, although it has changed now into a land of fear where you hesitate to sit down in a café or stroll in a shopping mall or board a bus for fear of being blown to pieces by a suicide bomber. Four years ago I travelled alone to Israel for a family wedding, and avoided catching buses; these days I would have to keep away from shopping malls too. The next thing would be to avoid sitting in hotel lobbies – a typically Israeli custom, watching the world go by and hoping to meet old friends. There are guards outside cafés, restaurants, super-markets, cinemas, and theatres, at bus stops and in market-places. Israelis are living in a state of siege.

However, this will never stop me going to Israel to sup-port my fellow Jews. Israel is the land to which millions fled for refuge from the countries of their birth, and they are still going there even though there is every chance that they or their children might get killed. I have family living in Israel whom I worry about constantly, and also Cardiff friends who have emigrated there over the years of Israel's existence. Perhaps this is the main way in which Wales and Israel differ: life these days is safer in Wales.

Either way, I shall continue to feel torn between being home in Wales and 'at home' in Israel among my fellow Jews, balancing my love for the Land of My Fathers against my love for the Land of my Fathers' Fathers.

X

WHERE AM I,
WHAT AM I DOING HERE?

The accounts of travel brought together in other chapters all suggest, in many different ways, that in spite of the difficulties, frustrations and sometimes dangers it can bring, travelling is essentially enjoyable and that overall travellers gain from their experiences of travel, even if this happens in ways they do not expect. So it seems only fair to use the final chapter to point out that travelling can also be a deeply negative, unpleasant or dislocating experience and that the only pleasure some travellers get out of it is in imagining themselves home again.

The pieces here differ from those in the previous chapters is another way also: whereas the other pieces describe the places or people of other countries or relate the events seen or experienced there, the experiences here (and in one piece, the place also) are firmly located within the writers' heads. Reality – whether it is threatening or gently dream-like – lies in what their own imaginations suggest to them.

The first piece, which gives a vivid picture of fear and loathing in New York (and presents an interesting psychological contrast to the picture of the city in 'Manhattan Spice'), is a reminder that the effect of travel crucially depends on the state of mind of the traveller, and that for someone visiting another country (especially for the first time) who is unprepared for the experience and sees their response to it as failing some sort of test, being in an unfamiliar place surrounded by unfamiliar people can be deeply disabling. The second piece dramatises the sense of emotional and psychological dislocation which being in completely unfamiliar surroundings can bring. It is probably significant that the women in both pieces are travelling alone.

In one case travelling produces a collapse into pure panic and a sense of the writer's own frightening insignificance; in the other it leads to a retreat into an imaginary world where her trancelike alienation produces physical collapse and decay in the hotel where she is staying and a realisation that everything in it is as much an illusion as the flowers made from coloured paper and plastic which she had thought at first were real.

In both cases, the demands which travelling has made on them are eventually too great, and for both of them going home offers not only a sense of relief at being in familiar surroundings but also a degree of emotional and perhaps physical refuge. By the end of both pieces the question is less whether the protagonists will get home safely than whether, when they finally arrive, they will have been so changed by their experiences of travel that home will not be the same any more.

Feeling Green in the Big Apple

HAYLEY LONG

My first nervous breakdown was so subtle that I hardly noticed it myself at the time. Eighteen and abroad for the first time, I sat very still in my YMCA cell and tried not to think about the sixteen storeys which separated me from street-level New York.

Something unfamiliar and uncomfortable was happening inside my head. This wasn't exactly what I'd expected – but then again, what exactly *had* I expected? I'd only ever been to London twice and on both those occasions I'd been under the heavy policing of a school trip, so they could hardly be counted as street-wise city experiences, could they? When it actually came down to it, I was forced to admit to myself that the nearest thing I knew to the big bad world was Cardiff, and where I was sitting now certainly wasn't Cardiff. This was Hell.

The weird feeling continued inside my head. Way down, deep in my mind, I registered a growing storm of panic and paranoia. All at once it struck me that I understood now what my Nirvana records were about. They *were* out to get me, after all.

I suppose that being from Merthyr had made me complacent. I'd always thought it could be a pretty dangerous place on a Saturday night after the pubs had closed – poverty and drink can sometimes do bad things to people after dark and it doesn't do to walk in the wrong places or rattle the wrong nerve-endings, so you have to be street-smart. Or *ffordd ffres*, if you prefer to speak *Cool Cymru*. 'I'm Elli Jones from Merthyr. I can handle myself.' Except that now I was having doubts. The only thing I was clear about was that I longed to be back there – sitting in St. Tydfil Square at throw-out time would be easy next to this. Because when all is said and done, Merthyr is nothing more than an outbreak of spots on the arse of humanity compared to New York. New York is the Black Death itself. I shut my eyes to think, as the feeling of paranoia inside me grew some more.

Whichever way I looked at it, it seemed that I had made a very big mistake. They had told me that Summer Camp would be fun. They had told me it would be a breath of fresh air after being cooped up in Aberystwyth for three terms. They had told me it would be the making of me. But they hadn't told me how to survive New York. And they hadn't told me I would have to spend the night on my own here. They had obviously been having a right bloody laugh at my expense.

I sat on the floor of my room and tried to get my senses back into some kind of order. Breathing fast, I began to divide and analyse the confusion of emotions in my head. I felt excitement. And amazement. And terror. How could it happen that I, Elli Jones, could step off a plane and suddenly be reduced to the size and significance of an earwig?

Looking out of my tiny window I screwed up my eyes and tried to focus on the back-street below. Four ageless figures in baseball caps were cutting up the alley on their thundering skateboards. The machine-gun sound of their boom-box sped up through the air to tell me to fuck off back into my room and quit staring at them. I did as I was told and turned my gaze in another direction so they wouldn't catch my eye and decide to murder me.

The day seemed unnaturally dark and, looking upwards, I discovered why. All around me were the blackened walls of countless skyscrapers which soared up into the heavens from every direction. Only a tiny square of uncluttered sky was left to greet the day and shed its meagre light on the city. I slid my window shut, locked my door securely and went down the fifteen flights of stairs to find comfort in the company of people who would be immeasurably more cheerful than I was.

In the hostel's common-room I found the people but not the comfort. As I pushed open the door I was confronted by the sight of two hundred young people sitting on chairs and pool tables, and felt my heart sink as four hundred eyes turned to stare at me.

'Glad you could join us,' said the bearded man at the front cheerfully. The four hundred eyes regarded me coldly for a second longer and then turned back to their original focus.

I sat down on an unoccupied area of floor-space the size of a postage stamp and quietly swore at myself for forgetting the Camp Programme Survival Talk. This could make all the difference between me pulling through and getting out of New York alive, or not. All around me the other students were busy scribbling down a long list of life-preserving Dos and Don'ts that the bearded man was reeling out with enthusiastic abandon. Don't hitch-hike. Don't join a religious cult. Don't turn left out of the main doors of the hostel. I sat in a blind panic and felt the paranoia in my head grow even more.

'. . . and finally – regarding bears. Should you be in a position where you are trying to escape from an imminent bear attack, never climb a tree. If the bear is a Honey Bear, he will simply run up the tree after you and eat you. If, on the other hand, he is a Grizzly he'll shake the tree until you fall out and *then* he'll eat you.'

The roomful of young people roared with laughter but, sitting at the back in my tiny square of space, I was able to register a frightening degree of earnestness behind the speaker's words. I swallowed hard to keep the bile from rising, made a mental note of the bear advice and felt, not for the first time, a sudden sentimental pang of *hiraeth* for my tough little town far away on the edge of the Brecon Beacons.

Vacation

DIANA GRIFFITHS

The hotel was massive, with marble floors, pillars and staircases. Chandeliers hung from high ceilings and exotic plants grew green and vagrant in corners, up walls and across climbing structures, to flower suddenly in strange wild clusters of sharp colour. Outside, below the tall windows and beyond the pool enclosure, lay the sea, flat and glittering like lemonade in the bright sun, or reflecting red as it set.

It was all hot and still. The guests were watchful, stumbling over the strangeness of language and custom in an alien land. They were mainly German and British, and they moved slowly together in the restaurant and across the long marble concourse after supper like horses and cows in the same field: different species respecting each other's space without acknowledging each other's existence.

On the second day she noticed everyone was making friends; tables for one were becoming tables for two, and tables for two rapidly grew into tables for four. 'Haven't *you* got any friends?' the waiter asked her, as she waited for a breakfast table. 'They aren't here,' she said, though when she thought about it later she couldn't remember any friends. That evening at supper she introduced herself to a young man sitting stiff and alone at the next table. He was German and neither of them spoke the other's language, but they got along well enough. After supper they heard the sound of music playing down one of the long stairways on another floor, and followed it.

And then they found the dancing.

Tangos, waltzes, quicksteps, charlestons, minuets and polkas, boleros, mazurkas; at first they watched, fascinated, as the performers swayed and swirled and never stopped or faltered. And then the dancers began to beckon and gesture to them until they found the urgency of the moment too hot to bear; their feet began to tap of their own will and without knowing how it happened the two found they had joined the dance. They danced all night until they were drunk with movement, until they realised that the music had stopped and saw that the dawn was breaking.

The next night they danced again, and then night after night, always in a different space in the hotel. After supper the music would start to play and they would follow it down corridors and staircases, through archways and tunnels, across barren deserts of floor, around odd corners they had never seen before, until they found it. When the music was upon them they danced, and went on dancing until they were exhausted. And the floor was always crowded with dancers who were every night always different.

By day they sat quietly by the pool or walked along the blue sea shore, gathering their energy until suppertime came round and the music began to play again.

And so time passed and time moved on, until one day there was a change in the weather and the wind began to blow.

Gently at first, it blew dry and hot across the sea from Africa, always in a miraculous constant exhalation without ever any pause or let for breath. Slowly, hotly, the wind rose, bending the tops of the palm trees and the orange trees; gradually it whipped the waves into an outrage till the sea rose up perpendicular, like a great blue horse with its white mane flying, making the horizon look greater than the hotel itself and the hotel seem to lean backwards. Even the swimming pool and the children's pool became dark restless hazards in the gale, and the guests shivered in spite of the warmth and stayed indoors, watching, for safety.

But there was no safety and no shelter and the wind would not be kept out. It gathered its forces for a slow persistent siege of the great hotel. Deliberately it crept and crawled through cracks and crevices in walls and windows, drying and weakening them. It pushed its way in and nosed around corners and then finally exploded down the marble concourse, scattering all before it. Dust drove through the air. Dust dulled the brilliance of the chandeliers and the staircases. Dust blew onto restaurant tables and sprinkled itself on the food. Dry leaves scattered behind the dust and lay at the foot of pale marble pillars. Dust.

And when the wind had died at last and the guests picked themselves up, she saw that every one of them was covered by a fine gauze of dust.

She found she was alone. She looked up at the ceiling which she could no longer see and when she looked down she too was covered in dust. It filled her ears and eyes with blur and lay on her hair like a veil.

At six o'clock she went to the bar for Happy Hour, but Happy Hour had changed its time. And in the bar were old men she had never seen before, bickering because they could not get a drink. The music had stopped and the Germans had long since gone.

When the time came for the end she found she could hardly remember the beginning. She wondered if she had the strength to make the return journey, she felt so worn. Dust and leaves still lay on the marble concourse where they had fallen. Some of the pillars had cracked. Lingering for a last look at the exotic plants climbing the walls, she saw that the clusters of flowers which had thrilled her so much at the beginning were made from coloured paper and plastic, stuck in among the greenery. Had it always been like that only she had never noticed?

At the airport they went straight to their gate. They could see the plane waiting for them across a blank of tarmac that stretched like a desert. They set off towards it but the further they went, the further away it seemed. They went faster and faster, but gained no ground. They were running now. Some fell, some tripped over those who fell, and many were left lying on the ground behind. When she glanced back for a moment, she saw that it looked like the picture of a battlefield. She left her luggage lying where it had fallen, and turned back towards the aircraft.

And then the wind started to blow again.

This time it sprang up quickly and fully-fledged; it was cooler and gentler than before and blew from behind them, urging them on towards the plane. They moved with no effort and soon there was a weightlessness about them. Some of them stopped forcing their legs to move and found they were still moving forwards, lifted off the earth by the power of the wind.

And cradled and lifted by the wind they had now entered the plane although she could not have said how or when it happened only that the wind had dropped, and she was suddenly aware of peace and azure and white all around them as the plane took off in a long straight streak across the sky and began its journey home.

Notes on Contributors

PAULA BRACKSTON grew up in Wales, spent some years away and now lives in the Brecon Beacons with her partner and two children. Her first book was an account of her horseback trek around Wales – *The Dragon's Tail*. She has recently completed an MA in Creative Writing with Lancaster University and is currently working on a novel and a screenplay.

LETITIA DAVIES was born in 1920 into a family with a long connection to the Raj. Her early years were spent with her grandparents while her parents' matrimonial problems were being resolved. She flitted between a convent in England and trips to a reorganised family in India. When that too collapsed, her mother, financially distressed, moved to south India where Letitia's education was completed. On the outbreak of war she enlisted in the Indian equivalent of the ATS as a cipher operator and served with Southern Army command in India and Ceylon. After the war she worked for a British engineering company in what is now Bangladesh. She was present throughout the horror of Partition and its aftermath. Married with one son, she is now growing old in Wales.

CYNTHIA HARRIS was born and educated in south Wales. She worked as a nurse and midwife in Iraq (when it ceased to be a kingdom and became a republic), and Bahrain (at the time of the six day war between Israel and Egypt). She also worked in Northern Rhodesia (now Zaire) at the time of the Congo disaster and in Ghana soon after independence when Kwame Nkrumah was its first president. She is now retired and living in Monmouthshire.

ELIZABETH HARRIS grew up over the 'other' side of the

north Wales border in the Anglo-Welsh culture of the Pres-
byterian church in Runcorn. She met her husband while they
were both studying at the Welsh College of Music and Drama
and settled in Cardiff, where she has lived for over thirty
years. She brought up a daughter and a son and taught in
secondary and special needs schools. She now helps with the
care of her three young grandchildren and enjoys writing for
pleasure and performing some of her pieces locally.

IMOGEN RHIA HERRAD is a freelance journalist and writer
based in London and Berlin. Born in 1967 and originally
German, she learned Welsh on the Lampeter Wlpan course
and has lived in Aberystwyth. She writes on travel and
historic themes for various German radio stations – in German
– as well as short stories and articles in English. To make ends
meet she also does office work as a temp or translator from
time to time. In 2002 she fell in love with Argentina and is at
present working on a full-length travel book about Patagonia
in English. She is also writing a detective novel in German, set
in a tango class in Buenos Aires. *Ym Mhatagonia* is dedicated to
the Cypriot poet Neriman Cahit, who suggested that Imogen
keep a diary during her travels. Without Neriman's encouragement, she says she would not have written this piece.

CAROLE MORGAN HOPKIN was born in Cardiff but brought
up and educated in the Swansea Valley. She graduated from
the University of Wales, Cardiff. However, an early diploma
course at Cardiff College of Art led to a lifetime of painting
and drawing as a commissioned artist in the UK and the USA.
Carole began her acting career with the Welsh National Opera
and Drama Company, which led to many West End appear-
ances. Having written since childhood she took up writing
professionally after a seven year stay in America, living in
New York, Florida and California. Back in her home town as a
freelance writer her most recent publications are with *Poetry
Wales*, *The New Welsh Review* and Gomer, who published *Full
Circle*, a biography of photographer Llew E. Morgan. Carole is

an Associate Tutor in Cultural Studies and Personal Development for the University of Wales, Swansea.

GWENLLÏAN JONES lives in Caernarfon but has also lived in Uganda, Kenya, Kuwait Qatar, Mauritius and Bangladesh, where her husband worked. She taught in some of these places. She has also travelled in India, Kashmir, Nepal, Thailand, Malaysia, Botswana and Namibia. She continues to travel now that she is a widow with two grown-up children. Her most recent trip was an embroidery tour of the Silk Road, in Uzbekistan and Turkmenistan. Her main interests are reading, writing and embroidery. She is the author of *Llythyrau Banglesh* (Bangladesh Letters), Gwasg Carreg Gwalch, 1998.

HEATHER JONES has travelled extensively in Greece since writing *Home Sweet Home* and says that almost every winter she threatens to leave her mid-Wales home for good! Her stories and poetry have been shortlisted in international competitions and as one of the winners of the Rhys Davies Award, Heather's work was published in a collection entitled *Mr Roopratna's Chocolate* (Seren). She is currently working on a collection of anecdotes about her travels in Greece.

MARIANNE JONES grew up on Anglesey. After graduating from university she taught English at a Japanese university. Before moving to Tokyo she lived in an area where no foreigner had ever lived before. She learned Japanese and helped to translate *Contemporary Japanese Literature*, which was published in 1972. She has also lived in Canada and taught English there. After returning to Britain she taught English as a second language, did a second MA and took up the post of Project Manager of the Japanese in Schools programme for the Welsh Office. After this she became Co-ordinator of the Japanese Resources Centre for Derbyshire County Council. She now lives on Anglesey with her husband. She has taught Japanese and Creative Writing there and is currently writing poetry and short stories. An earlier version of 'The First Alien' appeared in *Cambrensis* magazine.

BETTY LANE wears more than one hat. Most of her life has been spent as a potter and sculptor. She especially enjoys modelling portraits in terracotta, aiming at an accurate likeness of her sitters, but often capturing their inner selves as well. Her other favoured subject is based on astronomy. Phases of the sun and moon and exploding planets are designed and drawn onto wall panels to be coloured in luminous glazes. Her other hat is as a therapeutic counsellor. She returned to Cardiff University as a mature student to study for a degree in psychology and now runs a private practice from home. She lives with her partner, Eric – a jazz musician and graphic artist – in a Victorian house surrounded by a clutter of pots, portraits, pictures and piano music. These are some of the facets of her writer's persona.

CARMEN LANGE was born in Cardiff and worked for South Glamorgan libraries while studying for her librarian's charter at Gwent College of Technology. After what she describes as 'an *horrendous divorce*' she fulfilled a lifelong ambition when accepted unconditionally by the prestigious Institute of Archaeology, London. An honours degree in Near Eastern archaeology was followed by a Master's at the School of Oriental and African Studies to research the art and archaeology of China. A regular contributor to the Permanent Waves annual art exhibitions in Cardiff until she had major surgery, Carmen studies Chinese ink painting, makes lace and quilts. A Millennium Award Fellow and twice recipient of Arvon Foundation bursaries, she is a published poet and academic author. She is currently looking for sponsorship to complete her doctoral thesis on the origins of viticulture in ancient Turkey, and a publisher for her radically innovative fantasy novel in four volumes, *The Landsinger Chronicles*.

RONA LAYCOCK was born in Bangor. She now lives in Gloucestershire but her Welsh family and the places she has lived overseas heavily influence her writing. She married and moved to Tunisia in 1974 and started writing in a desultory way there and in Cairo. While living in Pakistan she visited the Buddhas of Bamiyan, in the times before the Russians or the Taliban took over Afghanistan, and was inspired to take her scribblings more seriously. Since then several of her poems and short stories have been successful in competitions and have been published in anthologies, helping to pay for the paper they were printed on. She teaches at Cirencester College and occasionally at Knuston Hall Adult Residential College, encouraging complete beginners to have fun with creative writing. She is currently writing a series of short stories set in Wales and a novel based in wartime Holland.

HAYLEY LONG was born in Ipswich, raised in Felixstowe, studied in Aberystwyth and now lives and teaches and DJs in Cardiff. The extracts included in this anthology were work in progress for her first novel, *The World of Elli Jones* (Bastard Books 2001). She is also the author of *Fire and Water* (Parthian 2004). A third novel is on the way.

MARY MILLINGTON originates from Oxfordshire and moved to Wales following eight years living and working at Greenham Common Women's Peace Camp (1982-1990). Mary took part in non-violent direct action there and at other nuclear bases, resulting in a number of short periods of imprisonment. She obtained employment after this, teaching in Brixton for two years, and also began to learn Welsh at the City Literary Institute in Holborn. It was savings from her work in London which enabled her to move to Cardiff in 1992 with the intention of continuing her Welsh studies. Mary now lives in Newport, Gwent, where she works part-time as a tutor to Welsh learners and is studying for a degree in Welsh at the University of Glamorgan. She has revisited Palestine twice since her initial visit and continues to be an active member of CND Cymru and the Palestine Solidarity Campaign.

PAULETTE PELOSI was born in Cardiff but a short time later moved to her parents' home town of Swansea. She was

educated at convent and grammar schools, but illness terminated 'A' levels and plans for a journalistic career. Chronic
illness was often a disruptive force in her childhood and
adolescence and continues to be so in adult life. In 1976 Paulette
collapsed at the end of her training as a State Registered Nurse
– a diagnosis of *Systemic Lupus Erythematosus* put a name (at
last) to the previous episodes of ill-health. Within two years of
diagnosis she became heavily involved in promoting knowledge about Lupus within a national charity, and went on to
become Public Relations Officer for the South Wales Lupus
Group (since retired). Paulette says that writing is one of many
personal survival tactics. She continues to live in Swansea
where she maintains a healthy sense of humour. Her Welsh
and Italian roots are both highly important to her identity.

SUSAN RICHARDSON is a poet, travel writer and freelance
creative writing tutor based in Cardiff. Her work has appeared
in a wide range of journals and anthologies in the UK, USA
and Canada including *Acumen, Orbis, Poetry Wales* and *The
Journal*, while her poetic drama, *Two Of Me Now*, is published
by Cecil Woolf in the Bloomsbury Heritage series. Recently she
was awarded a Churchill Memorial Travel Fellowship to
journey through Iceland, Greenland and Newfoundland in the
footsteps of Gudridur Thorbjarnardottir, an intrepid tenth/
eleventh century Norsewoman. Susan is currently writing a
travel book (working title *Three Islands and a Viking*) based on
her journey. For further information about her work please
visit www.susanrichardsonwriter.co.uk

ANN RUTHERFORD has now returned to live in her native
north Wales after several years living and working in England
and France. Twice married, she is happily divorced and shares
her house with a very large, very scruffy, deerhound lurcher.
She also has two grown up sons. Ann is currently working as a
counsellor and children's rights officer for a national charity.
For many years she has had a keen interest in the paranormal
and the UFO phenomenon and has undertaken extensive

research into associated subjects. She is now working on a book on the subject of UFOs.

JANE WILLIAMS (Ysgafell) (1806-85) described herself as 'Welsh by descent and long residence, but born in Chelsea'. She was a historian, a biographer, a book reviewer and a writer on social and religious issues to do with Wales; her best-known books are probably her response to the 1847 Commissioners' Report on working class education in Wales (*Artegall*, 1848) and *A History of Wales Derived from Authentic Sources* (1869). Her work on Betsy Cadwaladyr's autobiography (an attempt to raise money to help the ex-Balaclava nurse in her old age) remains an interesting early example of oral history and was re-issued by Honno in 1987 with an introduction by Deirdre Beddoe.

*

Sadly, some of the contributors to this book are not alive to see their work published. Some of them submitted autobiographical writings to Honno for a project organised under the auspices of the Welsh Arts Council in the late 1980s, and had died before work on this book began; their writings are now held in the National Library of Wales (full details are given in the Introduction). These writers include Freda Broadbank and Helen Wareing.

Stella Levey, whose article was written specifically for this book, unfortunately died before it went to press.

We would like to send our sympathy to their families and to express our thanks for their permission to publish these pieces, sometimes in a necessarily abridged form.

It has unfortunately been impossible to contact three of the contributors, Diana Griffiths, Joanne Routledge and Davena Hooson. We regret this very much and hope that they will be able to get in touch with us.

ABOUT HONNO

Honno Welsh Women's Press was set up in 1986 by a group of women who felt strongly that women in Wales needed wider opportunities to see their writing in print and to become involved in the publishing process. Our aim is to publish books by, and for, women of Wales, and our brief encompasses fiction, poetry, children's books, autobiographical writing and reprints of classic titles in English and Welsh.

Honno is registered as a community co-operative and so far we have raised capital by selling shares at £5 a time to hundreds of women all over the world. Any profit we make goes towards the cost of future publications. We hope that many more women will be able to help us in this way. Shareholders' liability is limited to the amount invested, and each share-holder, regardless of the number of shares held, will have her say in the company and a vote at the AGM. To buy shares or to receive further information about forthcoming publications, please write to Honno:

'Ailsa Craig'
Heol y Cawl
Dinas Powys
Bro Morgannwg
CF64 4AH.